THE PLUS FACTOR

THE PLUS FACTOR

A GUIDE TO POSITIVE LIVING

H.E. STANTON

To my parents who have given me so much

An OPTIMA book

© H.E. Stanton 1979

First published in Australia in 1979 by
Fontana Books
This edition published in 1988 by
Macdonald Optima, a division of
Macdonald & Co. (Publishers) Ltd

A member of Pergamon MCC Publishing Corporation plc

British Library Cataloguing in Publication Data
Stanton, Harry
    The plus factor.
    1. Self-actualization   2. Self-culture
    I. Title
    158'.1   BF637.S4

    0 356 15195 6

Macdonald & Co. (Publishers) Ltd
3rd Floor
Greater London House
Hampstead Road
London NW1 7QX

Photoset in Parliament
Made and printed in Great Britain by
The Guernsey Press Co. Ltd., Guernsey, Channel Islands.

Contents

Acknowledgments

My greatest debt is to the many writers I have read, and the many speakers I have heard, who have stimulated me to learn how to build a better life for myself. Some of these are referred to in the pages of this book; some are not for in many cases I can no longer identify the sources from whence my ideas have come. Special thanks are due to Julie Badcock whose comments on early drafts of the book helped greatly in its revision, and to Robyn Hill for her unfailing helpfulness in the typing of the manuscript.

1. You Can Change Your Life

REALITY VARIES FOR EACH OF US

Many years ago William Blake wrote: 'For some people a tree is something so incredibly beautiful that it brings tears to the eyes. To others, it is just a green thing that stands in the way.' In these words Blake summed up something I think all of us know and yet so often forget: we tend to see things not as they are but as we are. It seems that reality is not out there in front of us, able to be seen by everyone in the same way. Rather it is back in our heads behind our eye-balls.

Robert Hendrickson witnessed a car accident and is asked to testify in court about what happened. Four other people observed the accident and they, too, are called as witnesses. Robert gives his evidence, and then sits appalled as the other four tell their stories. So different are they from his 'truth', that Robert is convinced they are either lying or trying to make him look foolish. This may be so. It is far more likely that all witnesses are telling the 'truth' as they saw it. Each person is likely to have seen the accident differently depending on his physical position at the time the cars collided, his attentiveness, the sharpness of his eyesight and his past experience and feelings in similar situations.

Our perceptions of ourselves and of things that happen to us are so real that we seldom stop to doubt them. We accept the way things seem to us as the way things really are and we behave accordingly. That is, reality for each person is what it seems to be for him. Our failure to accept this is a most important cause of much human misery and breakdown in communication between people.

We all behave in terms of the way things seem to us at the moment of taking action. Behaviour is a matter of perception: and this word 'perception' means a lot more than just 'seeing'. It implies meaning, the particular importance an event has for the person who is experiencing it. Thus we behave in terms of the way things seem to us. Reality, then, can be defined in terms of how we perceive things. It follows that if we want to change this reality we need to change our perception. This gives us tremendous freedom. If reality was something objective, the same for all people, we would be unable to do anything about changing it. However, because reality is subjective, depending on how a particular person looks at things, it gives us tremendous power to manipulate our own behaviour. In fact, the purpose of this book is to outline various ways in which you can do this to make yourself feel better. Often we will go to a therapist who will show us how to make these changes in our own 'reality', but this is not essential. All of us have within us the power to act as our own therapist, to change the way we think.

Paul Swanson was moved by his firm to a new city. Actually, the name is fictitious, as are all others used in this book, but the person is real enough. He was very unhappy about the change. The new location was colder and wetter; it was too small to support the range of theatres he was used to; and people seemed to know everyone else's business. Paul was making himself miserable by dwelling on all the disadvantages of his situation, setting off a chain of negative thoughts, each one feeding on the one before. Eventually, he came to a realization of what he was doing to himself, and he determined to look for the good points of his new life.

He concentrated on the friendliness of the people, the beauty of the scenery, and the various pleasant social activities in which he could take a part. Once his thinking changed in this way, one positive thought generated another until he achieved a state whereby he enjoyed living in the new city. Nothing had really altered except the way Paul thought. However, the change in his thinking meant the difference between living happily and living miserably. Each of us has this choice, for I believe that most misery is self-inflicted and most happiness self-generated.

MOST MISERY IS SELF-INFLICTED

Perhaps you might find this view – that we are responsible for our own happiness or unhappiness – unacceptable. It does seem true, however, that thought creates after its own kind. Negative thoughts attract troubles to us just as positive thoughts attract pleasant results. This you can control. As Bristol has pointed out in the *Magic of Believing*, you can consider your mind as a room with a single door to which only you have the key. You decide whether you admit positive or negative thoughts through the door. If you persist in allowing entry to positive thoughts only, you will be able to banish the misery-provoking negatives.

This approach is far more effective than attempting to combat unwanted thoughts by 'making your mind a blank'. Emptying of the mind is a task most difficult to accomplish. However, deliberately replacing an unwanted thought by one you find more pleasant is not really difficult. In fact, after a relatively short period of conscious practice it becomes a habit, a habit through which you gain increased control over your mind. Sometimes it is true that the environment around us and the people with whom we interact can be influential in making us feel unhappy and in reducing our effectiveness as human beings, but most of the time our worst enemy is ourself. Emerson expressed this very well when he commented: 'Most of the shadows of this world are caused by standing in our own sunshine.'

Mary Thompson is a case in point. She came to me complaining of feeling depressed and unhappy because her son, who had married and gone to live in England, had not been writing to her. She claimed her son was making her unhappy through his reluctance to send her letters. This is one way of looking at it. Some other person is the cause of our misery. However, there is at least one other way of considering this particular problem. The real cause of Mary's unhappiness could be seen as her expectation of how a 'good' son should behave. In her view, he should be in constant contact with his mother who had sacrificed so much for him. It could be argued, then, that it was this woman's expectation that was the cause of her problem, not her son's behaviour.

If this view of the situation can be accepted, remedial action is fairly obvious: to help Mary change her expectations about her son's behaviour. In this way a new 'reality' is created. Such a change resulted in her accepting that her son's first loyalty was to his wife and that, as a mother, she no longer had the right to prescribe a code of conduct for him. If he chose to write to her that would be marvellous, but he really had no duty to do so. The actual situation was as it had been before, in that Mary still received no letters, but her perception of the situation had changed so that she no longer felt unhappy about it. She had chosen to change the way she thought and, by so doing, modified her feelings.

YOU CAN CHANGE YOUR ATTITUDE

If it can be accepted that our miseries are primarily self-inflicted, it follows that the greatest freedom we have is the ability to decide the attitude we will take to something. Lorraine Barrett discovered this. When her husband told her of his affair with another woman she developed anxiety symptoms, found it difficult to sleep at night, experienced bad headaches and stomach pain. She directed towards the other woman, whom she knew, a tremendous amount of hatred, but she felt fear too. In fact, she became frightened to answer the door or the telephone in case this other woman wanted to gloat over her. I was able to point out to Lorraine that her negative thinking was poisoning her life. It was not affecting the other woman, but she was making herself ill and unhappy. Actually, her hatred was giving the other woman tremendous power over her. This, of course, was the last thing she wanted. Realizing the way she was thinking was hurting no one but herself, she was able to assert control over herself. This process took some time, but she did succeed in returning to health, both physical and mental.

YOU CAN CHANGE YOUR THOUGHTS

If the first two premises can be accepted, that most misery is self-inflicted and that we have the freedom to change the attitude we take to something, it follows that the way in which we can improve the quality of our lives is through control of our thoughts. It is true that we are not responsible for the thoughts that enter our mind, but we are responsible for the thoughts that we allow to remain in our minds. We do have the power to control what we are thinking about. As Epictetus commented several centuries ago: 'Our life is what our thoughts make it. Men are disturbed not by things which happen, but their opinion of things which happen.' If you can change the way you look at things, you can avoid the misery that goes along with a negative viewpoint.

When you wake up in the morning, you may feel miserable and depressed for no apparent reason. At this point, you have a choice. You can continue to feel miserable, unhappily thinking about how bad the day will prove to be, how awful you feel, and how terrible life is. If you do think in this way, the chances are very great that you will have a thoroughly unhappy day because one negative thought triggers off another and another and another until you are thoroughly depressed. But you can change the way you feel quite easily by changing the way you think.

You can force yourself to smile and sing to yourself, although you do not feel like doing either; you can tell yourself that the day is going to be really good, thinking of some of the pleasant things which could happen. This is a real effort at first, but within a matter of minutes your mood will lift. You will be able to anticipate a day that is a lot happier than the one you would have otherwise experienced. Conrad Weiser, for one, obviously finds it easy to look forward to the wonderful things the day can bring:

Joy! A very beautiful word indeed. Maybe it just means that I like getting up in the morning because today has got to be the best day of my life, and there are going to be a lot of experiences I never had before. Maybe it means that I missed the world while I was sleeping and can hardly wait to get on with it again.

The choice is yours. For you are the only person who can control the way you think. It is your choice whether you waste hours feeling unhappy and miserable, or whether you change the way you look at things, refusing to waste time being gloomy. You can think of each day as a fresh new life, the only life you have, and refuse to ruin it by thinking negatively. Instead of letting the environment dictate your responses by making you feel irritable and unhappy, you can create your own internal environment of tranquillity by the way you think.

Sportsmen often face this problem when they perform badly and feel thoroughly miserable as a result. I have often had this feeling myself when I have been beaten in a tennis match through my own bad play. There is simply no enjoyment in playing a sport when you are constantly abusing yourself, disliking yourself because you are performing so badly. In tennis, it is possible to change your perception by seeing each rally as an entity in itself, once over to be forgotten. When each point is seen as something separate, poor play can be forgotten, but the well-stroked shot retained as a pleasurable experience. By dwelling on the positive aspects of your play you will generally enjoy the game far more. Actually you will perform a lot better, too, because you will not be fighting yourself over your bad play.

All I have said so far may seem obvious. You know it all. We already have far more knowledge than we need to help us live productive, successful and happy lives. The problem is not, therefore, attempting to acquire more knowledge, but to better apply that which we already have. My main objective in writing this book is not to tell you something dramatically new. Rather it is to outline ways in which your existing knowledge can be used more effectively to change your life in the ways you want to change.

2. Your Thoughts Have Power

THOUGHTS AND BELIEF

Much human wisdom is often epitomized in few words. 'All that we are is the result of what we have thought', said Buddha. 'What we believe, that we are', wrote W. L. Russell in *Peace and Power*. Developing a deep belief in the power of your thoughts can transform your life. Thoughout the ages, philosophers, sages and inspirational writers have affirmed that most of the limitations on man's achievements are due to his belief in limitation. We can only experience that which we believe possible and perhaps we are overly cautious in what we expect for ourselves.

Is it indeed true, as many have claimed, that man can be anything, do anything, and have anything if he is able to convince himself it will be so? Maybe this is going too far, but I find it a far more inspiring thought than one which sees man as hopelessly limited in what he can achieve. I believe we use but a small part of our mental and physical resources, permitting ourselves to be far less than we might be. John Tabb said it so well:

Every year that I live I am more convinced that the waste of life lies in the love we have not given, the powers we have not used, the selfish prudence which will risk nothing, and which, shirking pain, misses happiness as well.

I hope that, through reading this book, you will awaken, or perhaps re-awaken, to the knowledge of the power you have to avoid the wastage of life to which Tabb refers. Through controlling what you think you can transcend so many of the limitations you have placed on yourself. To permit yourself to do so you must believe it is possible. It is. Everything I write about is drawn from my own experience, from my own attempts to make the most of my potentialities. The principles I shall be talking about have worked for hundreds of people with whom I have been in direct contact as an educator and a therapist. There is no reason why they should not also help you gain more from life if this is what you desire. To achieve this you must believe it possible that you have within you the power to succeed.

Either you control your thoughts or you allow your thoughts to control you. It is that simple. Your dominating thoughts mould your state of consciousness which, in turn, determines how successful you will be in life. You have a choice. This is the key. You can decide *you* will choose the thoughts which are to dominate your mind. Deliberately you will place them there, resolutely returning to them time and time again despite distractions, temporary lapses, and periods of doubt. Or you will leave your mind open to the influences of your environment, to the people around you, the media, the 'experts' ready to tell you how you should live your life. Exposed to so many conflicting influences you drift, indecisive and doubting yourself. I repeat that the choice is yours. No one makes you think in ways that are harmful to you. You allow it to happen by refusing to take responsibility for regulating the food you feed your mind.

THE SELF-FULFILLING PROPHECY

Max Stone was a lonely man, uncomfortable when meeting other people. He 'knew' that people did not like him. They avoided his company, found him awkward to talk to, and were often quite hostile towards him. Max 'knew' this would always be the case when he mixed with people, and he was right. In his mind he had established a self-fulfilling prophecy, an expectation of what would happen in each new situation he entered. What he did not realize was that his own behaviour was provoking the very reactions from others about which he was so unhappy. Expecting people to avoid him, he showed in his own behaviour that he had no time for others. Anticipating that conversation would be difficult, he was awkward for anyone else to talk to, for he said little, communicating in grunts and monosyllables. Expecting hostility his whole body radiated aggression. His body said: 'Keep away from me. I'm angry.' Unless Max changes the way he thinks about himself, his behaviour will continue to repulse people, causing the very thing he wishes to avoid.

None of us are like Max Stone, are we? We do not create self-fulfilling prophecies in our own minds as a result of our dominating thoughts. Or do we? Do you ever get out of bed in the morning and bump yourself painfully on the door as you go to the bathroom? While still smarting from this little incident, perhaps you knock over a bottle of perfume or after-shave, spilling the contents all over the bathroom floor. 'Oh, oh, it's going to be one of those days', you might say.

It will be. With that thought firmly implanted in your mind, you are now on the lookout for all the things that will go wrong during the day. Your expectancy is for bad things to happen. Each time they do, you will gleefully affirm: 'I knew it was going to be one of those days.' You are a great prophet. All the good things that also happen to you are ignored because they do not fit your prediction. Now no one is making you think like this. You are doing it. Therefore you can stop doing it. If you would prefer not to waste the day feeling sorry for yourself you can do so by changing your thinking. Instead of concentrating on the negatives, look for the positives.

IMPROVE YOUR LIFE
THROUGH ATTITUDE CHANGE

Victor Frankl, in *Man's Search For Meaning*, claimed that man's greatest freedom is his ability to decide the attitude he will take to something. No life is so hard that you cannot make it better by the way you take it. To improve your life you must do more than accept this truth intellectually. Simply agreeing and saying it is an inspiring idea is not enough. You need to translate it into action, applying it to the myriad situations of everyday life. You decide to be positive, or you decide to be negative.

Ann Barlow disliked her sister-in-law. Her thinking about her was negative, resulting in a distant, frosty, hostile attitude whenever they met. The reason for this was simple. Whenever Ann made any alteration to her home, new drapes, new furniture, a different wallpaper, her sister-in-law usually made the same or very similar changes herself. Such slavish copying infuriated Ann who spent a lot of her time complaining about this behaviour. The more she complained the more negative she became. But no one was really forcing Ann to think this way. She had chosen the way she reacted to her sister-in-law's behaviour. I would suggest it was not a good choice because she became very upset whenever she thought about it, which she did quite frequently.

She could have adopted a different attitude. Imitation may be seen as the sincerest form of flattery: Ann could have taken the view that her sister-in-law was paying her a great compliment, acknowledging her superior taste and judgement, looking to her for guidance. If she had permitted herself to think in this way she would have felt positive about the situation, banishing the upset and unpleasant feelings. The actual situation would not have changed, just Ann's thinking.

I believe things are only worth what we make them worth. Two women can receive the same object as a gift. To one, the gift is appealing. She likes it. It makes her happy. To the other, it is unappealing. It brings her no pleasure and she thinks unkind thoughts about the appalling bad taste of the donor. The gift is the same. Only the reactions are different and the way we react is a product of our thinking. Control your thinking and you control your reactions. As Shakespeare put it: 'Nothing is good or bad in itself, but thinking makes it so.'

THE OPTIMIST AND THE PESSIMIST

The optimist sees opportunity in every catastrophy: the pessimist sees catastrophy in every opportunity. Each is wrong about as often as is the other, I suppose, but I suspect the former has a lot more fun in life. Also, through his positive expectancy, he is more likely to create the conditions he desires. He creates a receptive framework, attracting opportunities. My own experience has confirmed this time and time again. When I adopt an optimistic attitude about something, believing it will come right and work out the way I would like, positive things start happening. Opportunities open up which had not existed before. Or to be more correct, I had not recognized their prior existence. They had been there all the time but until my attitude was positive I was unable to see them. Our thoughts have an attractive power, like to like. Deliberately generate a positive mental attitude, imagining success, accomplishment, and a whole chain of pleasurable circumstances follows. Adopt a negative mental approach, concentrating on all the things you fear will happen and you initiate a misery-provoking chain culminating in failure.

Frequently patients come to me, affirming that I am their last hope. They have tried everything, but nothing seems to help them. Their belief lies in some form of magic. Someone to snap his fingers and make everything come right. They fail to accept their responsibility for their own behaviour. Typically they will concentrate on all the negatives that happen to them. When I quietly point out that some of the things they have been talking about also imply that positives have been present, they will virtually ignore my statement, continuing to take the completely pessimistic line. They are shutting the door on the very thoughts that could help lift them from their depression, preferring to pursue a line of thinking that must bury them deeper in the mire. Much of my work is aiding them to change the direction of their thinking, the hardest part being to start this process. Once a few positive thoughts are permitted to flourish, they generate others and the healing process is under way.

STOP SABOTAGING YOURSELF

What such therapy attempts to achieve is initially a reduction and finally a cessation in self-sabotage. Abraham Lincoln commented shrewdly that: 'Most folks are about as happy as they make up their minds to be.' Accordingly, the therapist assists the patient to see that, if he wants to leave his depression behind, *he* has to decide to change himself. He has to stop sabotaging his happiness through his own negative thinking. You do not need a therapist for this. You can do it yourself if you want to.

There is, however, another form of sabotage which must also be vanquished. This comes from other people. Unfortunately, the basic reactions of most people seem to be negative and critical, particularly when they are in contact with someone fired by enthusiasm. It has often been claimed that 95 per cent of people think in a predominantly negative fashion. How writers come up with such a precise figure rather puzzles me. Still, I think their basic proposition is correct. If you are to succeed in your efforts to change your life through controlling your thinking you will need to protect yourself against this damaging input. This is not always easy.

A patient of mine, Joanna Graham, was recovering from a nervous breakdown. Her progress was excellent for a few weeks, then she sunk back in apathy and misery from which I was unable to rouse her. Eventually the reason surfaced during a hypnosis session. Her husband, parents and in-laws were constantly feeding her a diet of depressing thoughts. She faced a barrage of comments along these lines: 'You're so pale and drawn, dear. You look so ill. Therapy is certainly not helping you. Just like Aunt Elsie, she never recovered, you know', and so on. A veritable litany of defeatism. With allies like this, who needs enemies? Once the cause of the problem had been identified, a very simple technique provided the solution.

Joanna, when subjected to the negative thinking of her 'loved ones', imagined herself slipping on a beautiful golden helmet. This covered her head completely, and most of her face. She 'saw' the negative thoughts bouncing off, unable to penetrate her protective headpiece. At the same time she generated her own positive thoughts, providing a more rewarding diet which restored her to health quite quickly.

In chapter 3 I shall elaborate more fully on this concept of mental imagery, but Joanna's example illustrates a very important point. Most of us spend too much time thinking about the thoughts of others rather than creating our own thoughts. By doing this we tend to become the servants of other people rather than taking control of our destinies. This is disastrous when these outside thoughts are negative in direction. It is very difficult to think of yourself as a winner, as a success, if you allow other people to tell you how hopeless you are. Perfect you may not be. Who is? But hopeless you are not, unless you really believe this of yourself. As you read on, I trust you will start regarding yourself in a more optimistic light, armouring yourself against the destructive influences of a negative environment.

MASTERY OF YOUR ENVIRONMENT

You can assume a considerable degree of mastery over your environment as you become more practised at governing your thoughts. Most of us, not realizing our power, are slaves to wandering thoughts and feelings. This is one reason why the world seems to be so chaotic. However, once you do realize your power and use it, you will feel a sense of mastery, being able to reaffirm with George Meredith: 'The wind that fills my sails propels, but I am the helmsman.'

In an era when many psychologists claim that we have no real freedom, that what we are and who we are is completely determined by the circumstances of our birth and early environment, it is gratifying to know we do retain considerable ability to change ourselves in ways we desire. We do not have to remain under the control of our environment. Become conscious of your own requirements, selecting the things you will permit to influence your mind. Tell yourself only those things you desire to be true of you. Make your environment work for you and not against you.

Pauline Ronaldson has been requested to attend her son's school. The purpose of this visit is to discuss, with the headmaster, her son's disruptive classroom behaviour. As she enters the headmaster's office she feels vulnerable, inadequate, overawed. Memories of the past flood into her mind and, to some extent, she again becomes a timid, self-doubting schoolgirl confronting an all-powerful, punitive figure. She has allowed her environment, both the external one of the headmaster and his study, and the internal one of her own fearful thoughts, to control her. As a result she feels inferior, giving the headmaster considerable power over her. She does not have to do this, for she can change her internal environment by blotting out the negative, fearful thoughts with positive, strengthening ones. After all, we can only think of one thing at a time so the most effective way of banishing a damaging thought is to substitute one which is more welcome.

Let us consider some possibilities. The headmaster is just another human being. Therefore, he is not perfect in any shape or form. On occasions he is just as silly, irrational and unreasonable as the rest of us. He is prone to foolish decision, and to insensitive handling of both students and parents. Not all the time, of course. On other occasions he is wise, compassionate, efficient and intelligent. He is, in short, like Pauline, another human being. As a result of his position, he may be assumed to have a certain expertise, but this does not necessarily carry with it the right to exercise control over a parent. This will only occur if the parent allows it to occur. If Pauline tries thinking along lines such as these, she will be in a far better position to resolve the problem of her son's behaviour. She will be exerting mastery over her thinking, her internal environment, and by so doing turning an initially untenable situation into one more to her advantage. When John Milton wrote these words: 'The mind in its own place and in itself can make a heaven of hell, a hell of heaven', he was expressing this idea in a much stronger form. It is no less true for that.

FAITH CAN HELP YOU

Reference to Milton's verse brings to mind the question of faith. You either believe in the power of the mind or you do not. Everyone has faith in something. Some have faith in failure, sickness, accident and misfortune. When you are exhorted to have faith, remember you already have it. The real question is: how are you using it — constructively or negatively?

We assume that people with a religious faith are at an advantage here. This is not necessarily so. Often people pray only as a last resort. They turn to God for help when all else fails, an attitude denoting a lack of confidence that their prayers will be answered. Fearfulness and expectancy of failure are not good companions of prayer. Those, however, whose religious convictions are strong and whose faith is genuine do not approach prayer in this way. They confidently expect positive results, and their faith is a powerful shield against the invasion of negative thinking.

The feeling that we are protected by a Supreme Being is tremendously comforting. This is so, irrespective of whether such a Being exists or whether protection is actually extended to human beings. Combating negative input through readings from the Bible has proven effective for many people. Perhaps the twenty-third Psalm, 'The Lord Is My Shepherd', is the most popular in this context. Faith in God as an ever-present help in trouble, as offering support and everlasting mercy, helps us cope with misfortune more positively. Possibly the most effective of all formulas in this sense is that of Epictetus: 'I am always content with that which happens, for I think that which God chooses is better that what I choose.' If you can really believe this to be so, nothing will disturb your serenity. Everything that happens must be for the best because God has willed it so.

Too facile? Too simple? Perhaps, but having met people who do believe in this way, I am greatly impressed with the peace they seem to have found. We are too apt to reject as ridiculous anything that does not conform to our own prejudices. If some way of thinking, some form of faith, helps a person cope more happily with life, I am all for it. Each of us has to find his own way and we should be very reluctant to criticize the path trodden by other searchers.

THINK IN TERMS OF PAY-OFFS

It is really a matter of results or pay-offs. If something works for you, it is worth pursuing. If not, no matter how good other people tell you it is, try something else instead. Considering the pay-off you get from your actions is related once again to the messages you give yourself.

John Sutherland saw a girl at a party. Human chemistry being what it is, he thought he would like to meet her. Before this quite natural impulse had a chance to be translated into action, John started thinking about his own inadequacies as a human being. He was unattractive and shy. Often he stumbled over words, blushing as he did so. A whole catalogue of such failings occupied John's mind. By dwelling on these he convinced himself that there would be no point whatsoever in approaching the girl because she would certainly reject him. His assumption was that all the faults of which he was so painfully aware would be immediately apparent to the girl on first meeting. This is quite an unrealistic attitude to take. It is also very common, particularly among young people who are highly over-critical of their own physical appearance.

Most of us, in fact, make much harsher judgements of ourselves than do others whom we meet. As far as John is concerned, what he has done is conclude he is so inadequate that the girl would have nothing to do with him. She would say 'no' to his advances. Therefore, he makes no attempt to meet her. He could talk differently to himself, considering that if he approached the girl and was refused he was no worse off than if he had done nothing. On the other hand, the chance exists that she might say 'yes'. Perhaps she, too, was good at telling herself how awful she was and would be flattered that someone thought her attractive enough to approach.

Through taking action, John has some chance of a favourable result, a 'yes' answer. If he avoids doing so, he has no chance of this whatsoever. One way there might be a pay-off; the other way there certainly will not. Perhaps John should read a little Shakespeare: 'Our doubts are traitors making us lose the good we oft might win by fearing to attempt.' Self-trust is the secret of success, and this you develop through the messages you tell yourself, taking action in ways that maximize your chance of a positive result.

THOUGHT-SWITCHING

John's main error was concentration on himself. A rather effective way of coping with such excessive self-preoccupation is through diverting the attention elsewhere. It is preferable, in an interpersonal situation, to concentrate on the other person. Focus on her, listen carefully, show your interest. By so doing you can forget yourself. You also create a very good impression for everyone likes to feel they are sufficiently interesting to be listened to attentively.

This diverting of attention idea works well in many situations. You are blazingly angry at your wife. If you remain in her presence you are likely to attack her, either physically, verbally, or both. Go for a walk. Hit a punch-bag. Shout at the dog. Snarl at yourself in the mirror. Anything at all that diverts attention. Channel your anger into activity. It helps you control your thoughts.

Perhaps you are trying to lose weight, yet you are thinking about eating. First, move out of the kitchen, away from the sight of food. Find something to do that has no relation to eating, preferably something that demands your intense concentration. As you lose yourself in this activity, you forget about eating because your thoughts are otherwise engaged. It is like the soldier who attacks an enemy outpost without realizing he has been wounded. When the flurry of action is over he collapses. Or the business man, feeling tense and anxious, thinks he must have a cigarette. He is in a meeting, however, where no smoking is permitted. If he would take a few deep breaths he would relax and the need to smoke would pass. Once again it is a matter of changing what you think. Allow your thoughts to remain on eating and you will feel hungry; divert them to something else and you forget about eating.

This is a process which could be labelled thought-switching. It does not necessarily involve any physical activity as in my examples above. Whenever you become aware you are thinking negatively, making yourself miserable, you deliberately switch your thoughts to something more pleasant. Suppose you are waiting for someone. He is late. You become more and more impatient. As your tension mounts you start thinking uncharitable thoughts about the person who is causing you to wait. To what point? Your fretting will not make him come any faster. All you are doing is starting a chain of negative thinking which results in anxiety and strain. Use the time pleasantly. Dwell on that magnificent beach holiday you had last year. Remember the exultation you felt when you sunk a hole in one. Experience again the excitement you felt at a superb concert. Remember, you decide what you think, so do not blame someone else if you make yourself miserable.

This is really a matter of taking responsibility for the thoughts which are in your mind. Further, because the way you think profoundly influences your actions, it is also taking responsibility for your own behaviour. Wayne Dyer in his book, *Your Erroneous Zones*, puts this idea well when he suggests that we ask ourselves the question: 'What am I doing to make myself unhappy?' That is, we, rather than some outside agency, are likely to be the cause of our own unhappiness. This attitude is in marked contrast to that adopted by most of us when we ask the question: 'What is making me unhappy?' If the question is asked in this way, we are giving up personal responsibility for our state of mind, transferring it to the environment in which we live. By so doing we relinquish any chance we might have of controlling our minds. Instead we wait for someone else outside ourselves to do whatever is necessary to make us feel better. We are likely to wait a long time. As Dyer has pointed out, if you blame the injustice of the environment for your problems you will never change until injustice goes away. It never will, of course, so you are doomed to your misery unless you accept personal responsibility for your thoughts and your own behaviour. One way of doing so is the thought-switching procedure described above.

You can help this process by using a companion technique called thought-stopping. As soon as you realize that you are thinking negatively, say 'stop'. Say it loud if you wish, otherwise silently. Alternatively, you could imagine a neon sign flashing on and off in your mind saying 'stop'. Because this word carries such prohibitive connotations, it serves to pull us up short. This gives us the chance to more easily change the direction of our thinking. The change I suggest is to replace the negative thought with its opposite. If the former continues to re-occur, keep switching. Soon the disturbing thought loses its power. It does not matter particularly if at first you do not believe what you are telling yourself. You soon will.

Sometimes when I am being badly beaten in a tennis match, I find myself thinking: 'This chap is too good for me. I'm playing woefully today. I'm feeling tired. I have no hope of winning this game.' If I permit myself to continue this line of thought I will beat myself. My opponent will not have to do much at all because I will have convinced myself I cannot win. Here is where I say 'stop'. Then I switch deliberately, telling myself: 'I'm starting to play better. He can't keep this up much longer. I'm feeling fitter all the time.' When I first think this way I do not believe it. How could I? I am being annihilated. Yet, within a few minutes, as I keep up the flow of positive thoughts, I do start playing better. Because of this my opponent misses more shots. I still may be defeated, but my opponent now has to accomplish this. I am not going to do it for him. Often, it is this positive mental attitude that is the deciding factor in matches where individuals or teams are evenly matched. Success in sport, as in life generally, may be more a matter of mental attitudes than of physical capacity.

Thought-switching takes effort. It will not just happen. You have to work at it. In his fine book, *Shōgun*, James Clavell has Kiku, the courtesan, remember some advice she has been given:

Always remember, child, her first teacher had impressed on her, that to think bad thoughts is really the easiest thing in the world. If you leave your mind to itself it will spiral you down into ever increasing unhappiness. To think good thoughts, however, requires effort . . . so train your mind to dwell on sweet perfumes, the touch of silk, tender rain-drops against the shoji, the curve of this flower arrangement, the tranquility of the dawn.

In *The Human Machine*, Arnold Bennett says much the same thing. The mind must be trained through an effort of will. This is to be achieved through practising concentration. Bennett suggests that we should spend half an hour each day forcing the mind to concentrate on a single idea or topic. No 'breaks' are to be permitted. For that period of half an hour, the mind must be made to ignore every idea except the one we have selected for attention. The aim of this practice is to see the mind as external to the supreme force which is ourselves, and in subjection to that force so that we can turn it on and off a particular subject at will. Such control is what thought-switching is all about.

SYSTEMIZE YOUR THOUGHT CONTROL

You can make the whole thought control process very systematic if you so desire. Jean Wallace's case demonstrates how this might be done. After eight years of marriage, she found she was deriving no enjoyment from her sexual relationship with her husband. To her, intercourse had become a dull, dreary chore which she felt it was her duty to perform. She could solve her problem by ceasing sexual relationships entirely, but felt this to be unfair to David, her husband. The answer she sought was one which would enable her to recapture a feeling of sexual pleasure. If she could achieve this, intercourse would become an enjoyable experience instead of something to be endured. One way of doing so would be to increase the number of thoughts she had about sex as a pleasurable experience. In particular, Jean could relive in her imagination past sexual episodes which had been good.

For one week we kept a record of her thoughts. Pleasurable sex did not appear at all. On those occasions she did think about sex, the context was very negative. The first step, then, was to establish a goal: thinking pleasurably about sex. Next, this thinking was to be linked with some high probability behaviour, something Jean did regularly each day. We decided on sitting down and standing up, an action she normally performed frequently during the day. Now what Jean did was to think about enjoying sex whenever she sat down, and again immediately after she stood up. No great time period was involved. Just a couple of minutes on each occasion, yet by the end of the day she would have had forty or fifty pleasurable thoughts about sex. Many of these were of past episodes, but an increasing number were anticipatory, thinking of enjoyment to come. Action is a result of our thoughts, and Jean was conditioning her mind towards sexual pleasure. As a result, with her mind controlling her body, she began to look forward to sexual intercourse, no longer seeing it as something to be endured.

This systematic approach may be interpreted as a re-programming of the subconscious mind, which has often been compared to a computer controlling our body processes and our emotional states. The 'computer' data it works on to perform this function are your thoughts. To effect this change in yourself, then, you re-programme your computer by deliberately controlling the information you feed in. This is what Jean did. The result was a change in her attitude as her thoughts altered the message in her computer. Whether this way of looking at the action of the subconscious mind is true or not is difficult to ascertain, but in the next chapter we shall look at its functioning more closely.

3. Suggestion & Your Subconscious Mind

THE POWER OF SUGGESTION

Behind all the discoveries of psychologists since Mesmer . . . lies one of the great truths about the mind. It may be expressed as follows: if the mind really accepts an idea as true, and if the idea is reasonable, it tends, by means of unconscious processes, to actualise itself or come true. To bring about the entry of an integrating idea into the mind, so that the idea may 'come true' is called treatment by suggestion. (L. D. Weatherhead, *Psychology, Religion and Healing*).

By using auto-suggestion, i.e. suggestions we make to ourselves, we can help ourselves to change in the directions we desire. Such suggestion may be verbal, as: 'I shall be calm and confident, relaxed and happy', or it may be a mental image, such as imagining oneself on a set of scales with the scales showing the weight one wishes to be. Each of us has this tremendous power to assume control over our lives through the use of suggestion, feeding into our minds the words and images embodying the self we wish to be.

One way of making use of this power is through a conditioning process. Oz Mandino has provided an excellent example in his book *The Greatest Salesman In The World*. He suggests certain attributes such as love, persistence and a sense of humour, as essential to success in life, and sets out a method by which the reader may achieve these. Each of the valued attributes, described as a habitual response to life's situations, has a chapter to itself wherein, with considerable repetition, it is described. The reader is asked to read each chapter three times daily, silently on arising in the morning, silently after the midday meal, and aloud before retiring at night. This procedure is to be followed for thirty days before the next chapter is treated in the same way. The purpose of such an approach is, in Mandino's words:

Herein lies the hidden secret of all man's accomplishments. As I repeat the words daily they will soon become a part of my active mind, but more important, they will also seep into my other mind, that mysterious source which never sleeps, which creates my dreams, and often makes me act in ways I do not comprehend.

YOUR 'TWO' MINDS

It is the subconscious mind to which Mandino refers. Effective use of suggestion does seem to be linked to processes taking place below our normal level of conscious functioning. Our conscious mind, using information supplied by the five senses, concerns itself with functions such as reasoning, thinking and planning. Our subconscious mind would seem to operate by means independent of the physical senses, using intuition as a method of perception. It controls involuntary operations in the body such as breathing and digestion, serves us as a memory storehouse and is the home of the emotions. Although we really have no scientific proof of their existence, it almost seems as if man has two minds, each endowed with separate attributes and powers, and able to operate independently.

Perhaps the most important difference between the 'two minds' relates to the question of suggestion, a finding derived from research into the phenomenon of hypnosis. Although we do accept suggestion in our normal, waking state, it is subjected to critical scrutiny and evaluation by our conscious mind. This is why negatively inclined people rarely change their attitudes. They combat incoming information of a positive kind with an array of reasons why it will never work. It does seem to be a fact of life that people are exceptionally good at advancing all the reasons why new projects, new ideas, must fail. They are far less able to recognize the success possibilities inherent in many worth-while suggestions.

However, when we allow ourselves to relax and enter a hypnotic state, our normal critical faculties are suspended and we are able to accept incoming suggestions more readily.

Should we so desire, resistance is still possible and, in fact, quite easy, but the essential fact remains that suggestion works far more powerfully when we are relaxed with our physical senses in relative abeyance. In such a state, not only do we accept suggestion from someone else more readily, we also accept our own suggestions more easily.

This is also the rationale for self-hypnosis and auto-suggestion. If it can be accepted that man's two minds possess independent powers and functions, it follows that a person's subconscious mind is just as amenable to suggestion provided by his own conscious mind as it is to that provided by the conscious mind of somebody else. Herein lies the basis of the mind–power thesis expounded in chapter 2. Our conscious mind can control our subconscious mind by the suggestions it feeds in, and if we choose to make these positive in nature such an approach to life soon becomes habitual. This is because the subconscious mind does not reason inductively. It does not consider a variety of known facts and from them derive general principles. Instead, when given a general principle to start with it will reason deductively to derive all legitimate inferences. The subconscious mind will accept the general principle as true and proceed to implement it through all the means at its disposal. There is no need for you to spell out how this is to be done; all that is necessary is to implant the suggestion.

With my patients who desire to improve their self-confidence, for example, I help them imagine themselves behaving in the way they would like to behave. They visualize themselves in various situations acting confidently, displaying poise and self-possession. I do not tell them how they will achieve this desired goal but only implant the suggestion that this is the way it will be. The patient then practises such imagery for himself, either at night just before falling asleep, or at a time when he retires to a quiet place and relaxes himself by using one of the techniques to be discussed below in this chapter. Once the subconscious mind accepts the suggestion, in this case conveyed through mental imagery, it will convert it into reality through the absolute control it exerts over the functions and sensations of the body.

SELF-PROGRAMMING
THE SUBCONSCIOUS MIND

When the individual takes the responsibility of deliberately controlling his subconscious mind, he has embarked upon a process of self-programming. He thinks of the way or ways in which he would like to be different and deliberately turns over to his subconscious mind the achievement of such objectives. He then diverts his conscious mind to other business.

This self-programming is facilitated if a relaxed state is used for the implanting of suggestions. Using Baudouin's term in *Suggestion and Auto-suggestion*, there is an 'outcropping of the subconscious' at such times when we are drowsy, dreamy or in reverie. They occur, of course, quite naturally just before we fall asleep at night and again immediately after awakening in the morning. At such times it is advisable to repeat verbally, either to oneself or aloud, the suggestions and to imagine scenes which depict you behaving in the way you wish to behave. That is, it is helpful to see yourself as if you already possess the particular quality, such as confidence, or something material such as money.

Various formulas have been described by which this technique can be used to achieve wealth. Basically they all involve thinking of yourself as wealthy, telling yourself you are wealthy and using various techniques to make concrete images representing wealth. For example, it is possible to visualize the things you can purchase with money. See yourself with the car you want. Imagine coming home from work in this car and garaging it. Vividness of imagery is important, so you not only 'see' the car in your imagination, but 'hear' the engine, 'feel' the wheel, the upholstery, 'smell' the new-car odour.

Another approach is to create a treasure map of the thing you want. Cut out pictures showing objects like the one you want and paste them on a sheet of paper. Write affirmations around them claiming that they are already yours. Behave as though you believe this completely. Focus your mind on the thing you desire as you drift off to sleep, repeating its name over and over again, telling your subconscious mind to get it for you. Of course, you can visualize money itself, rather than what it can buy for you. 'See' your bank-book with a figure of $100,000, if this is your goal, 'feel' yourself handling a cheque for this amount payable to you.

It is up to you to create your own visualizations and suggestions, whether they be aimed at acquiring wealth or whether they be directed towards some other goal. However, their effect will be many times more powerful if you use the naturally occurring periods when the subconscious mind is more accessible. Keep suggestions short and simple, repeating them often. Weatherhead portrays picturesquely the importance of so doing when he says:

We all have a critical apparatus . . . likened to a policeman on traffic duty. Some traffic he halts and turns back. Some he allows to pass only with reluctance. Some he unhesitatingly signals to come through. So, when ideas are presented to the mind, the critical apparatus, or policeman, rejects some, lets others through with only half-hearted approval, and welcomes some. I can imagine that a cyclist approaching a town might more easily elude the vigilance of a policeman if the attempt to do so were made in the half-light of early dawn or the dusk of evening . . .

The early morning, when we waken, the evening just as we drop off to sleep, are the best times for suggestion to be made by the mind . . . I can imagine, too, that a policeman on duty who refuses, say, a cyclist the first time, might ultimately let him into the town if he presented himself again and again. So, if an idea is repeated again and again, the critical policeman is more likely to allow it into the mind. (*Psychology, Religion and Healing*)

Weatherhead mentions that period when we are dropping off to sleep as being particularly appropriate for the placing of suggestions in the mind. An extremely powerful form of visualization, termed 'remaking the day', may be fruitfully employed at this time. It involves your thinking back over the events of the day, congratulating yourself on those which have gone well, and 'remaking' those which have not turned out as you would have wished. As you visualize each 'good event', allow yourself to bask in the warm glow of achievement. As you visualize the 'not-so-good events', wipe them from your mind as if you were rubbing them off a blackboard. Then you replay the experiences, visualizing them the way you would have liked them to occur. Treat separately each 'not-so-good-event' in the same way. Probably you will fall asleep well before you finish, but that is of little moment, for your subconscious mind will be working on this positive input while you slumber. What you are actually doing with this technique is making your day perfect. You are conditioning your mind to see yourself as you want to be.

CREATE YOUR OWN RELAXATION STATE

At other times, you can create this state of drowsy reverie for yourself. Retire to a quiet place where you will not be disturbed. Make yourself comfortable by loosening clothing and settling into a chair. Alternatively, you may wish to lie on a couch or the floor. There are many methods you can use for inducing deep relaxation. One of the simplest is to breathe deeply and slowly, repeating the word 'calm' with each exhalation. Another is to think of each part of your body in turn, feeling it 'let go', becoming limp and heavy. If this should prove difficult, tense a particular muscle first and then allow it to release. Most people prefer to start with the feet, working up one leg at a time, feeling the limbs becoming increasingly heavy. Then the body, stomach, chest and shoulder muscles all let go. Feel yourself melting down into the chair or couch, letting go more and more with each breath. Your breathing will slow down, becoming deep and regular. Each arm, beginning at the fingers, relaxes too, then the neck and facial muscles, until all is at rest. Although this particular technique is very popular slow, progressive relaxation is not necessary for many people who can achieve the same effect by 'letting go' the whole body at once.

Other approaches involve shutting the eyes and counting, feeling yourself going down and down with each count. A variant on this method is to imagine yourself in a building, on the tenth floor, waiting for a lift to take you down to ground level. The lift arrives, the door opens and you go in, turning to face the front. As the lift door closes, you focus your attention on the panel displaying the floor numbers: number ten is illuminated. Smoothly, comfortably, pleasantly the lift descends and as it does you see the appropriate floor numbers lighting up on the panel: 9, 8, 7, 6, 5, 4, 3, 2, 1, G. With each number you feel yourself letting go more and more, drifting down and down, deeper and deeper into rest and relaxation. When you reach the ground floor you are very, very relaxed, peaceful and calm.

Should you so desire, you can then imagine yourself leaving the lift, crossing a hallway and entering a quiet, tastefully furnished room, one in which you feel very much at ease. In this room is a very comfortable chair, the most comfortable in which you have ever sat. As you imagine yourself sinking down into this chair, you let go completely, Alternatively, you could visualize yourself sinking down into a couch or the carpet on the floor. However you care to structure your mental images, the basic idea remains, that of creating your own world, of making it completely real inside your mind. In this way you let go the outside world and create your own environment of relaxation.

Inducing eye-closure by fixing your eyes on a particular object can also promote relaxation. As you rivet your gaze and your attention on an object, preferably something shiny, you tell yourself your eyes are becoming heavier and heavier; you are drowsy, relaxed; you need to blink with increasing frequency; it is just too much effort to keep your eyes open. As your eyes close, you suggest that all your muscles are letting go and you allow yourself to drift into a state of calm reverie, very similar to that you feel just before drifting off to sleep at night. Have no fears about awakening when you wish to do so. A simple count to five, suggesting that when you reach five your eyes will open and your mind and bdy return to normal in all ways will be quite effective. With these procedures, do not force yourself in any way. Just allow yourself to let go. If this is difficult at first, keep practising and relaxation will become easier and easier.

OVERCOME YOUR LIMITATIONS

The variety of suggestions you can give yourself when in this relaxed state is limited only by your imagination. It has been proposed, in fact, that our only limitations are those we set up in our own minds. To overcome such self-imposed restrictions it is necessary to use your imagination constructively, visualizing things as you want them to be. Such an approach is dramatically opposed to the more common negative use of the imagination whereby we 'see' things as we fear they will be.

A patient of mine, Diana, developed a phobia about air travel. Every journey was a nightmare. She remained tense, anxious and sick with worry, straining her senses to detect any slight change in engine noise, any hint of tremble in the plane, any faint suggestion of disaster. Her imagination conjured up vivid pictures of the plane crashing in flames with her resultant death. This is what I would describe as negative use of the imagination. It produces no gain, only worry, nervous tension and misery. To overcome this problem Diana learned how to relax and drift into the dreamy sort of state similar to the feeling we get before we fall asleep at night. In such a state she was able to imagine herself travelling by plane, calm, peaceful and serene, actually enjoying the journey. This did not occur all at once, of course.

Initially I had her visualize a really happy, relaxing scene to which she mentally shifted whenever she felt at all nervous during the course of her imaginary plane trips. At first these journeys were quite short and Diana frequently switched to her happy scene. Once she calmed down, she returned to visualizing the plane journey. After these sessions she was able, in her imagination, to travel from Sydney to London without any feelings of anxiety at all. She remained relaxed and serene. Several weeks later she actually made this journey without re-occurrence of the previous unpleasant feelings.

This is no isolated case, and points up the wisdom of these biblical words: 'The thing I feared has come upon me' [Job 4.14]. If we constantly dwell upon the things we fear will happen, we create a negative expectancy in our mind, ecouraging their very occurrence. The antidote is the positive use of the imagination, the creation of the desired image of ourselves as we want to be. Define the goal you wish to achieve and write out a scene implying that this 'dream' has already become a reality. Then place yourself in the appropriate role and, in imagination, live it to the fullest extent, bringing in emotion, speech and action. In addition, duplicate your scene, either briefly in words or as a drawing on a number of small cards. Carry one of these with you in your pocket, wallet or purse, and place others beside your bed, in your bathroom, on your desk. By concentrating on one mental picture at a time in this way you will achieve rapid results.

This approach has obvious applicability in the area of sport. See yourself performing the way you would like to. Obviously you cannot, by so doing, generate abilities you do not possess, but you can help yourself to use those you already have. As most of us employ but a fraction of our potential ability, the use of imaginative suggestion should lead to substantial improvement. This can be instantaneous.

Before the last football season, a local club sent me a player who had lost confidence in himself. In previous years he had been one of the team's best players but, in pre-season practice matches, his form had been so poor that he would have been dropped. He saw me the evening before the last practice match and, in imagination, I helped him relive his best games. He 'saw' himself replaying his longest kicks and his most brilliant marks. Images of strong, courageous, confident play filled his mind. At the end of the session he imagined himself being congratulated for a great game in the practice match. When he left me he was virtually quivering with eagerness to get on to the field. Next day he was the best player on the ground. Not always can such immediate results be expected, but rapid improvement is very common indeed.

BELIEF IS IMPORTANT

Elmer Leterman said it well when he claimed: 'We are what we accept ourselves as being. We can be what we convince ourselves we can be.' This convincing is what we do when we use suggestion, both verbal and visual. However, it is not enough to do so with the wish that it should happen. We should work towards the cultivation of a deep, abiding belief that it will be so. It is easy to say that you should believe; it is harder to tell you how to achieve this. A wish takes place upon the surface of the mind whereas a belief is created in its depths. It becomes part of you. To help belief become habitual think about your own experience of the existence of subconscious powers. Consider the inexplicable healing that occurs due to faith; the opportunities that present themselves as you think positively; the way things come so much easier when you mentally rehearse them beforehand, seeing obstacles melting away. There are sources of power within us we seldom use. Look for positive things happening. Focus on these and your belief will grow.

Take a very simple example. I found if difficult to get out of bed in the morning. Not too uncommon a complaint really, but one to which I am not usually addicted. After this occurred for a couple of weeks, making me feel lethargic and 'flat', I suddenly realized how ridiculous the situation was. I knew I had the power to solve my problem so easily. I had just forgotten. The next evening, as I lay in bed I imagined myself waking in the morning. I 'saw' myself full of energy, vitality, eager to get on with the day's activities, looking forward to the marvellous things which were going to happen. In my imagination I threw back the bedclothes and bounded out of bed. A trite example, perhaps, and I am not suggesting that everyone would necessarily want to bound out of bed each morning. Still, I like to. It makes me feel better, and by the use of suggestion given during the relaxed state I changed my behaviour from that which I did not want to that which I did. It is that easy. Within you, you have this power to change yourself in those ways you want to change.

Perhaps you can see this as a form of de-hypnotization. Maltz, in his popular book, *Psycho-cybernetics*, has pointed out how easily we can be hypnotized by a false belief about ourselves. So often this false belief stems from other people. I really believe that our limitations are, in the main, not inherent but have been accepted through the suggestions of others. If we are less than we ought to be as a result of uncritically accepting negative suggestions, we can enhance ourselves through giving ourselves positive suggestions in the way outlined in this chapter.

Julie Kennett, a teenager who consulted me because of a weight problem, illustrates this point. As a child she had been continually told by her mother that unfortunately she would be fat as a result of her heredity. Julie's parents and grandparents were all overweight. The cause was not heredity, though. Plain over-eating was the problem. However, Julie accepted her mother's suggestions, consumed the excessive amounts of food provided for her, and put on weight as expected. In a series of four sessions, she learned to relax and to imagine herself weighing the weight she wanted to be and looking the way she wanted to look when she had lost the desired weight. In particular, she saw herself in a variety of sleek new outfits, enjoying the way she looked in these clothes. In addition to this mental imagery, I gave Julie suggestions relating to moderate, healthy eating habits. She repeated both visual and verbal suggestions each evening before going to sleep and before every meal. Her weight gradually decreased as the power of her own suggestions overrode the negative influence of those implanted by her mother.

SUMMING UP THE PROCEDURE

To sum up, then, to make the most effective use of your inherent power to change yourself use this procedure. First, decide on a specific goal, something you desire very strongly. Perhaps it is money, self-confidence, or simply to stop biting your nails. Second, use either a naturally occurring period when the subconscious mind is most accessible, such as just before you fall asleep at night, or create such a situation through the use of relaxation techniques. Third, suggest to yourself the things you want. Make these suggestions brief, clear and very positive in tone. Then imagine yourself already in possession of the attributes or things you desire. Visualize your goal as already achieved. Fourth, repeat this procedure many times, setting a specific date for the actual realization of that which you suggest. Finally, strengthen your suggestion by acting as if it has already come true. If you really wish to appear decisive to other people, commence acting that way. This is a matter of conducting ourselves as if we were such as we wish to be. As Shakespeare said: 'Assume a virtue if you have it not.'

4. Coping with Anxiety

SYMPTOMS OF ANXIETY

Have you ever experienced the fear that something awful is going to happen? This is a sensation often associated with anxiety, made worse by the fact that you do not know why you are frightened. Danger threatens but its source is unknown to you. Or perhaps you worry about everything. People who are anxious spend much of their time worrying, sometimes over past events, occasionally over current incidents and often over anticipated events. It is this constant worry over the memories of the past and the fear of the future which makes living in the present so miserable for many people.

Lynda Henderson is such a person. On their wedding anniversary, her husband made her a gift of a mink coat. After the first flicker of pleasure, Lynda began worrying about whether it would be stolen. Would she dare to wear it out? Someone might accidentally burn it with a cigarette, or spill alcohol over it. Then she became suspicious of her husband. Was he doing something about which he felt guilty? Surely the coat was a means of relieving his feelings of guilt. Lynda Henderson is a very unhappy person, unable to derive any enjoyment from life because she is her own worst enemy.

Anxiety manifests itself in so many forms: the girl who blushes uncontrollably when she meets people; the man who sweats profusely whenever he talks with his employer; the business man who trembles whenever he has to address his stockholders. Elaine Smythe is a constant visitor to her doctor. Her symptoms are many and varied, including stomach cramps, blinding headaches, a suspected ulcer, an irregular heartbeat, and vomiting. No organic malfunction has been identified. She exists on tranquillizers and anti-depressants like millions of her fellow sufferers, yet is still prey to anxiety. She continually worries about her health, escalating each new physical symptom into a deadly illness. Should her throat feel sore she dwells on this until she is certain she has a cancer; should she feel listless, she knows she is a victim of leukaemia.

Thousands of children, and many adults too, experience the trauma of examination anxiety. They know their work but, faced with the examination situation, their minds go blank, their palms sweat, their hearts race, and they perform badly. Generalizing more widely, the same syndrome can be identified in any test-like situation: the man applying for a job, the new bride cooking her first meal, the nervous mother bringing her first-born home from hospital, all worry about how they will cope, and feel anxious about the outcome. The list of such situations is endless and by now you would have probably identified at least one of the illustrations as part of your own experience. Perhaps it is now appropriate to ask why we have such symptoms. Why do we experience these feelings called anxiety?

Anxiety involves fear, though we do not really know what we are frightened about. It is vague, free-floating and nebulous. We feel something is wrong but are unable to identify the cause of our unease. Under such conditions our brain is alerted and, through the endocrine system, adrenalin is produced in our bodies. This hormone affects virtually every part of our body and creates the symptoms described above. Our muscles tense, ready for fight or flight. Such tension frequently causes trembling, and sometimes a painful ache. Changes occur in our blood vessels. Those carrying blood to the muscles relax, thus increasing the flow, while others contract so that little blood reaches areas such as the face. This is the explanation of expressions like: 'His face blanched with fear.' Because additional blood must quickly reach the muscles, the heart beats faster thus increasing its pumping action. Our breathing speeds up to provide the extra fuel we need to ready ourselves for flight or fight. All these changes are valuable in helping us cope with any danger that threatens. Other changes are not so functional. Because adrenalin affects all muscles, our digestive system is unnecessarily stimulated, often causing cramp, diarrhoea and nausea. The body's water balance changes too, leading to excessive sweating and dryness of the mouth.

You will recognize the description given above, I think. The problem is, however, that our body is now ready to cope with the threatened danger which, in the case of anxiety, does not exist in any specific, identifiable form. We are prepared for a fight or to flee most effectively, but we have no target for these activities. Gradually we may calm down as the wave of anxiety passes, the flow of adrenalin into our system subsides, and our bodies return to a more restful state. However, if this process is frequently repeated our bodies tend to remain in a more or less permanent state of tension, a readiness to cope with a threat which never seems to materialize. When this occurs, the symptoms described above in this chapter are the result. In *Stress Without Distress*, Hans Selye has pointed out that most illness is caused directly or indirectly by chemical imbalance in the system due to stress or tension which is, in turn, mediated through glandular malfunctioning.

WHY DO WE EXPERIENCE SUCH SYMPTOMS?

The usual reason for these symptoms is fear, though the causes of such fear are so varied that an attempt to catalogue them would require a book in itself. Perhaps the most important would lie in our childhood experiences when we are so dependent on others to satisfy our needs. To achieve this end we virtually have to buy love with our good behaviour. It seems so unfortunate that throughout our society, and particularly in respect to the way children are reared, the basic principle is to ignore things that are done well and to punish things that are done poorly. The child who is constantly upbraided for his inappropriate behaviour fears that he will lose the love of his parents and, by so doing, will no longer be protected and looked after. Some of us are fortunate enough to outgrow this fear as we recognize our power to provide for ourselves. Others remain fearful thoughout their entire lives. At times this fear is repressed, buried deep in our minds, unrecognized consciously, but at other times it surges forth, creating the sudden anxiety that floods our bodies with adrenalin.

Such childhood-induced fear may be the reason why we may attempt to act the role of someone we are not. Jack Robinson was a real man's man. He drank heavily and often, until he was sick; he was continually out with the 'boys' rather than at home with his wife and family; and he was the dedicated womanizer, complete to the almost compulsive boasting about his many conquests. Yet Jack was a deeply unhappy man, tense, frustrated and anxious. During our therapy sessions I regressed him to his childhood and many early events were recalled. It became quite apparent that both Jack's parents held before him their ideal of a real man – tough, hard drinking, hard playing. Weakness or softness of any sort was despised and their definition of such behaviour seemed to include politeness, consideration for others, interest in the arts and a desire for solitude.

As a child Jack preferred his own company, was unassertive, and found his chief enjoyment in reading and music. However, he quickly learned that such behaviour roused the anger of his parents. They made it quite plain they were ashamed of his 'sissy' attitude. To avoid rejection Jack forced himself to play a role which was foreign to his real self. In his adult life he had continued this role, yet remained a man at war with himself. Once he was able to recognize the cause of his present behaviour he was successful, over a period of time, in re-orientating himself so that he could live in harmony with himself. When he achieved this, his anxiety symptoms disappeared.

As I have stressed in earlier chapters, negative thinking is a prime cause of fear. Most of the difficulties which people experience in life exist more often in their imagination than in actuality. Yet, as I said above, what you imagine has tremendous reality for you, whether fantasy or not. These negative creations of your mind kindle fear leading to the now familiar anxiety symptoms. The limitations we place on ourselves are part of such negative creations and are a fruitful source of anxiety conflict.

This point is well made by Russell in *Peace and Power*, where he discusses it within the context of what he calls the mastery-submissive conflict. Russell sees the peace and strength of normal life as dependent on avoidance of the conflict between the desire to succeed and the fear of failure. Attempting to serve our best needs, the mastery instinct strives to overcome obstacles and to achieve our goals. The submissive instinct also attempts to serve our best interests by avoiding tasks which we fear are too difficult. The desire to achieve stimulates the mastery instinct while doubt, anxiety, fear of failure stimulate the submissive instinct. The result is anxiety conflict. In Russell's words:

If we are fearful and anxious about whether we can achieve success in an undertaking or attain the most cherished hopes of our life, then the submissive instinct *knows* we cannot. In a misguided attempt to conserve our energies, it flashes the red light and cries 'Halt!' The mastery instinct shouts 'on to victory' and the fight is on.

As I look back on my tennis career, I see the truth of these words. So often, in a winning position, I played safe because of doubt in my own abilities. I knew I should be aggressive, putting pressure on the other player, but instead preferred to wait for him to make the mistakes. Sometimes he did; many times he did not and I let victory which was mine for the taking slip away. I was fearful of failure, of missing shots, of making errors and these fears paralysed me into playing timid, ineffective tennis. If you consider your own experience you will, I am sure, find this mastery-submissive conflict operating in so many areas where you feel anxiety. Now I realize what is happening I am in a position to avoid the conflict. I do this by the conditioning process I described in chapter 3 whereby I continually feed into my mind the positive affirmation that I am a winner, that I am confident, determined and aggressive. To this I couple mental imagery, 'seeing' myself playing the way I want to play. I do not always win, but I am far happier with my game now that I no longer fight an internal conflict.

WHAT CAN WE DO TO COPE WITH ANXIETY?

It is of primary importance to understand what is happening. When you understand that the cause of your anxiety is an over-supply of adrenalin in your system, you are in a position to defuse the situation and help yourself. One way of so doing is to recognize the symptoms engendered by the first surge of adrenalin, realize what is happening, and go with the feeling, letting it pass over you. In Frank Herbert's science fiction classic, *Dune*, his hero, Paul, says: 'Fear is the mind killer. Fear is the little death that brings total obliteration. I will face my fear. I will permit it to flow over me and through me.' By acting in this way you avoid the long-term anxiety caused by worrying about the symptoms generated by the first adrenalin surge. You realize that you are not sick or dying, that there is a perfectly understandable reason why you feel the way you do. If you go with the feeling, refusing to respond with panic, it will pass quite quickly and you will return to normal. Conversely, if you respond with more fear because of the symptoms you feel, you greatly worsen your condition so that, increasingly, you suffer long periods of anxiety.

This is what happened with Margaret Webster. During menopause she suffered the discomforts of occasional dizziness, hot flushes, sweating of the palms, headaches, and a more rapid heartbeat. These symptoms terrified her to such an extent that she lived each day in a state of acute anxiety. Once she realized what was happening to her, that her panic-stricken concentration upon her symptoms was creating most of her trouble, she was able to cope quite successfully. She was aided in so doing by the relaxation-suggestion technique outlined above (p. 29). At the onset of her symptoms she remained calm, turning her attention to relaxing imagery instead of concentrating on the peculiar things happening in her body. As a result these became nothing more than slight discomforts which provided no interference with her normal mode of living.

USE MENTAL IMAGERY

There are many mental images you may use to help yourself in this way. It is a matter of experimentation until you find those which work best for you. A tranquillity room, for example, has wide appeal. This idea, and those which follow, may seem a little strange at first, but many people have derived great benefits from playing such 'mental games'.

Imagine a room furnished just the way you would like it to be, decorated in colours inducing relaxation. This room should be one in which you can feel serene, calm and peaceful. When you feel tension building within you, think of yourself approaching the house containing your room, opening the door, and entering. Imagine yourself going into the tranquillity room, shutting the door behind you, closing out the world, settling yourself comfortably and letting go. Feel the peacefulness flow through you, washing away all the tension. With practice, the whole procedure may take only a minute or two, though you might well prefer to relax for a longer period than this. Of course, your place of tranquillity does not need to be inside. Personally, I imagine myself floating around a beautiful swimming pool on an inflatable mattress. As I look up at a cloudless blue sky and feel the warm sun on me, my tensions drain away so effortlessly, so quickly. A restful garden or a quiet beach are other possibilities you may consider.

The red balloon technique is another 'mental game' found useful by many people. Imagine you are outside, somewhere you feel relaxed and at peace with the world. You are alone. The day is superb, a beautiful blue sky and the temperature just as you would like it to be. At your feet is a wicker basket, its lid open. Into this container you imaginatively unload all your unwanted feelings of anxiety, depression and gloom. Cleanse yourself of these, experiencing a sense of joyous rebirth as you do so. See the unwanted feelings, visualized perhaps as a muddy, dark ooze, filling the container. When you feel completely cleansed, close and fasten the lid. Imagine yourself moving a few feet away to where a huge red balloon is attached by cord to a peg in the ground. Holding the cord you untie the balloon, carrying it across to your basket and attaching it to the handle. Then you let go of the cord, watching the balloon rise higher and higher in the air, taking with it your unwanted feelings. Soon it is but a tiny red speck against the blue sky. It disappears. With it disappear your tensions, worries and gloom. You have just let them go.

Introducing humour into mental imagery can help too. If you can laugh at the pictures you invent you will not stay anxious for long. When angry, for example, think of yourself with a funnel on the top of your head, the sort of funnel you see on old-time steam engines. Imagine yourself pulling the cord activating the whistle attached to this and, as you do, see clouds of black smoke puffing out the top. This is your anger, black and sullen, but it is difficult to stay this way for long in the light of the rather farcical image of yourself puffing smoke out of your head.

You can use the same technique when other people intimidate you. In chapter 2 I described the awe a parent feels during an interview with her child's headmaster. Such an attitude hinders useful communication and can easily be overcome through imagining him in a ridiculous situation. Perhaps he could be 'seen' sitting at his desk dressed in long red flannel underwear, a feather growing out of one ear. Do not think I am just being unkind to headmasters. The same de-dignifying process can be used with anybody, be he politican, medico, lawyer or academic, who takes his position too seriously.

LIVE IN THE PRESENT

If you honestly examine your worst fears you will usually find them to be concerned with anticipated future events. The writer worries: 'What will happen if I lose my skill with words?'; the wife agonizes: 'What will I do if my husband leaves me?'; the student trembles at the thought: 'What will happen if I can't cope with the examinations?' Such anxiety has a common element, the 'what would happen if' syndrome. It is this fear of the future, together with worries about the past, such as: 'If only I had not invested in the stock market', that makes our present so difficult.

Yet it need not be so, for no one forces us to do this. We choose to do so; just as we can choose, if we prefer, to live in the present. Concentrate on the present moment. If you do, you will probably find that nothing is worrying you at this instant. Possibly it is too much to ask anyone to continually live in the present moment. It is not too difficult, however, to live one day at a time. Horace, as early as 65 BC expressed this concept tellingly when he wrote:

Happy the man – and happy he alone
He who can call today his own.
He who secure within can say,
Tomorrow do thy worst – for I have lived today.

Today is all we can live. The past is gone; we cannot change it; the future has not yet arrived. All we have is today, and we can choose to live it as a complete life in itself. That is why it seems such a waste, if you wake up feeling low, to allow yourself to remain in that state all day. You have wasted a lifetime. So often something goes wrong first thing in the morning and you say to yourself: 'It's going to be one of those days', and it will be, of course, as I pointed out in chapter 2.

There is, however, a simple cure for the early morning blues. Look at yourself in a mirror and smile. Then sing. Does this sound silly? It is not, though when I first tried it I certainly did not feel like smiling. Yet within a couple of minutes I felt like singing instead of wasting my day, my life, in feeling miserable, I enjoyed the day. Every day is a new life to a wise man, so the choice is yours to make of it what you will. It has been suggested that every day should be passed as if it were to be our last. This is good advice. So, too, are these words penned by Robert Louis Stevenson: 'Anyone can carry his burden, however hard, until nightfall. Anyone can do this work, however hard, for one day. Anyone can live sweetly, patiently, lovingly and purely till the sun goes down. And this is all life really means.'

We can do things for twelve to sixteen hours that would appall us if we felt that we had to keep them up for a lifetime. Like a bridge, man is designed to bear the load of the present moment, not the combined weight of a year at once.

AVOID TAKING OVER
THE PROBLEMS OF OTHERS

That is, incidentally, an excellent reason for not taking onto your shoulders the problems of other people. If you derive satisfaction from sharing the worries of others, helping them cope with their troubles, that is one thing. It is quite another to allow yourself to become distressed and distraught over problems which are not really your own.

Leslie Bodler did so to an extreme degree. Never did she miss a radio or television news programme, nor did the daily newspaper ever escape her attentive eye. Being retired, she was able to spend a lot of time worrying about the terrible things which were happening all over the world. As we know, news reporting is often concerned with unpleasant events, natural disasters, wars, terrorism, murder, and other forms of violence, so Leslie had an abundance of material about which to agonize. The plight of unfortunate people, wherever they might be found, oppressed her thoughts, their problems becoming her problems. This behaviour could perhaps be construed as admirable if some benefit stemmed from it, but this was not the case. Neither the people with the problems nor Leslie derived anything positive from her agonizing. For Leslie, her news-devouring behaviour resulted in depression and misery. Unable to do anything to help the oppressed of the world, she simply chose to make her own life very unhappy.

Fortunately, the solution to Leslie's problem was simple. She adopted my suggestion that she set each Monday aside as her 'news day'. On that day she read her paper and listened to her newscasts as usual. For the rest of the week she was to resolutely resist the temptation to engage in these activities. At first, she found this very difficult to do, but gradually it dawned on her that most of the terrible problems of one week had faded out of the news by the next week. They were no longer important. The realization enabled her to change her attitude, allowing her to let go of her obsessive desire to make the world's problems her own. An exaggerated example? Perhaps, but most of us are very prone to take on the problems of others. Often we do this fully aware of what we are doing. At other times we are manipulated by other people presenting *their* problems to us as if they were *our* problems.

Criticism is frequently the means through which this manipulation is effected. Gerald Kingsley was highly critical of his wife's love-making. With monotonous regularity he accused her of frigidity, unresponsiveness and insensitivity, making her very aware that he was left completely unsatisfied by her performance. His wife, Ruth, did not enjoy making love with Gerald, finding it very difficult to raise any enthusiasm at all. Accepting her husband's evaluation, she saw the fault as entirely her own. She had a problem, sexual inadequacy. After almost two years of living with this problem she consulted me in an almost despairing manner, feeling there was really nothing anyone could do to help someone as frigid as herself.

It became obvious very early in our first therapy session that the wrong person had come for help. To conceal his own lack of interest in sex, his own feelings of inadequacy, his own unwillingness to spend time in giving his wife pleasure, Gerald had projected it all onto Ruth. Unfortunately, as with so many other women, she had accepted her husband's evaluation. Gerald had the problem, not Ruth, yet she felt it was all her fault and that it was her responsibility to change herself, her responsibility to find some solution for their sexual maladjustment. This is no isolated case and it raises the more general point of how we might cope with criticism which so often is used to pressure us into doing things we do not want to do.

COPING WITH CRITICISM

Possibly the best book I have read dealing with this problem is *When I Say No I Feel Guilty*, by Manuel Smith. He points out how often when we try to do the things we want, we allow other people to make us feel guilty, ignorant or anxious. This is how we are manipulated, through the evocation of these three negative feelings. When we were children and we did not do what others wanted us to do, we were trained to feel one or more of these emotional states. Naturally we felt bad as a result, and did what was required of us to gain release from the anxiety, the guilt, or the feeling of being stupid. Thus, we were trained to accept someone else's 'shoulds', 'musts', and 'oughts'. In adult life, because of this childhood training, we are still easily manipulated into accepting other people's 'shoulds', usually through the mechanism of criticism. If you are not behaving in ways which the other person sees as appropriate, you are criticized. That is, it is wrong for you to act in the way you are doing. You 'should' behave in some other way which is 'right'.

Criticism can be constructive, of course, helping us to develop our potentialities more fully. Yet, I feel most criticism is essentially negative and destructive, designed to manipulate people and put them down rather than being offered in a positive way. To handle such negative input we need to develop certain protective skills. Our normal reaction to criticism is primarily defensive. We tend to deny it, thinking up plausible reasons for our behaviour. Then we counter-attack by pointing out certain deficiencies in the person making the criticism. This usually does not work, the result being a heated 'slanging match' with the criticized person often submitting to the other person's 'shoulds'.

A more constructive approach, which is most effective in turning off the criticism, is simply to admit that there is probably some truth in it. As human beings we are far from perfect, so by admitting this we are probably being quite realistic. However, once you forget about denying criticism and say something like: 'You're probably right. I am rather untidy', or 'Yes, I have made quite a mess. I can understand you're annoyed', you virtually take all the wind from your attacker's sails. There is not much mileage in his continuing to criticize you when you agree with what he says. As you accept your errors and faults quite openly your attacker's criticisms abate, fading away to mumbles, for he has nothing to fight about. There is no resistance at which to pound away.

The interesting thing that frequently occurs is that as you

admit your lack of perfection such as 'I did forget to pick up those clothes at the dry cleaners. How stupid can I be?', your erstwhile critic consoles you, stoutly declaring that you are not stupid at all. It may not always work out so well, but through your refusal to act defensively, and through your ready agreement with criticism, you defuse situations which often become very unpleasant.

Another very important thing to keep in mind when coping with criticism is to react only to what the other person says. It is very easy to read all sorts of implications into the simplest of questions. 'Do I have a clean shirt to wear?' only requires a very simple answer, hopefully: 'Yes. It's in the top drawer.' However, it is possible to interpret the question as a criticism of your housekeeping capabilities and to react very defensively. 'Of course you've got a clean shirt. Don't I always slave my fingers to the bone keeping you looking nice while you go off to lunch with your female clients. It's a pity I don't get more appreciation for the things I do for you' and so on. The question might have had a critical intent, but it is your choice whether you rise to the bait or not.

If you refuse to respond to anything else other than the words actually spoken, you will turn off a great deal of criticism. Besides, often you will be projecting your own feelings onto an innocent question or statement, reacting defensively to criticism which was never intended. Coping with criticism in the ways outlined above can lead to a quieter, happier life, turning off much of the stress which makes us anxious. Another way of doing so involves the gentle art of meditation.

MEDITATION CAN HELP

In previous chapters I have talked much about the value of relaxation as an aid to positive conditioning of your mind. It is also of tremendous importance to your control of anxiety. You cannot be relaxed and frightened at the same time. The relaxation techniques described above (pp. 27, 28) will not be repeated here. Instead, I would like to consider the use of meditation as an antidote to anxiety. Personally I find it difficult to identify the boundaries between relaxation, hypnosis and meditation. Many attempts have been made by adherents of each persuasion to distinguish their particular method from those of others but, to me, they seem to have so much in common that such efforts leave me unconvinced that there is a distinction. As I briefly outline some of the more popular meditative techniques I think you will observe many similarities with those I have titled 'relaxation'.

Before doing so, I would like to pause for a moment to consider the question: 'Why bother?' What is to be gained through such procedures? According to practitioners, the benefits to be gained are many, varying from changes in body processes to improved creativity of thought, to the curing of drug addiction. In particular, virtually every report, anecdotal or experimental, stresses the tension-reducing quality of the meditative process. Meditators are said to recover from stress more quickly than non-meditators; they report feeling 'protected' from the strains formerly experienced at work or home; and they claim a lowering of their anxiety level. Millions of people throughout the world do meditate on a regular basis as part of their normal routine of living. When questioned about this procedure practitioners almost unanimously include anxiety reduction as a reason for beginning meditation and for its continuation.

Basically there are three different approaches to meditation. The first of these is concentration meditation which involves focusing the mind on an object, either real or imagined, such as a candle; a sound, such as the mantra 'om'; a word, for example, 'calm'; or an abstract idea such as 'justice'. A second approach is the way of emptiness, whereby the practitioner focuses on stillness, emptiness and quietness of mind, detaching himself from the consciousness of his environment in order to attain a state of pure receptivity. Observation meditation is the third approach. This involves simple awareness of and attention to whatever emerges from within, with no attempt being made to control the direction of consciousness. All three methods are a deliberate attempt to separate oneself for a brief period of time, from the normal flow of daily life. The person who meditates seeks quiet and stillness, turning off the conscious mind as far as possible. In meditational exercises the common features are: (1) sitting alone or with a small group in a special quiet place; (2) keeping all external sources of stimulation to a minimum to avoid distraction; and (3) maintenance of special posture, either the lotus position or sitting upright in a chair with erect spine and little body movement.

Perhaps the two meditation methods most widely used in Western society to achieve anxiety reduction are: (1) concentration on a sound, and (2) concentration on one's own breathing. A common form of yoga meditation practice involves the use of a mantra, which is repeated over and over again. This mantra is normally a word of significance, such as the name of a god, or one which creates favourable sound vibrations. Possibly the most common is 'om' (pronounced aum). This may be repeated aloud or silently. Whenever the meditator realizes his awareness is straying he gently returns his attention to the mantra. In its most currently popular form, that of transcendental meditation, the practitioner silently repeats his mantra, specially selected for him by his instructor, for two periods of twenty minutes duration each day. The most appropriate times are considered to be before breakfast in the morning and before the evening meal. As the meditator, eyes closed and comfortably seated in a chair, repeats his mantra, he gradually drifts into deeper and deeper relaxation. The theory is that as he does so his mind flows freely, drifting in the direction of pleasing things. As long as such thought continues effortlessly and dreamily it is allowed to continue, but as the meditator realizes that he is starting to think consciously, he returns to his mantra. This may occur repeatedly during a single session as stress is released. After the twenty-minute period has elapsed, the practitioner sits quietly for two or three minutes before allowing his eyes to slowly open.

A variation on this theme has been introduced by Benson in his book, *The Relaxation Response*. He feels the mantra of significance is unnecessary and that any word will do just as well. Words such as 'one', 'calm' or 'flower' are suggested, but even your own name may be used. After all, the reason for repetition of a word is to help break the train of distracting thoughts, so Benson does have a point in maintaining that any word is just as effective as a mantra. You need not, of course, limit yourself to a single word. Your preference may be to use a phrase or a sentence, perhaps one taking the form of a positive affirmation. My own patients have found the sequence: 'I am calm, relaxed, confident and happy' particularly beneficial, both as a meditative mantra and as a means of relaxing themselves in their daily lives when subject to a stressful situation. As in conventional yoga meditation, the practitioner sits comfortably in a quiet place, his eyes closed and his body relaxed. Breathing through his nose, he says his word or affirmation silently as he exhales. This may be continued for ten to twenty minutes. Benson warns against meditating for a period longer than this, suggesting that you open your eyes occasionally to check the time. He also encourages the meditator to adopt a passive 'let-it-happen' attitude so that relaxation can occur at its own pace. Distracting thoughts are to be ignored, attention being brought back continually to the word.

The next step Benson suggests is a combination of sound, in this case a word, with concentration on breathing. A simple Zen Buddhist technique which has proven both popular and successful may help you achieve this. Sit with your head and back straight and erect; your hands resting easily in your lap, with the left-hand palm facing inward on the right palm. The tips of the thumbs touch lightly. Eyes may be closed or open. If you prefer to have them open, fix your unfocused gaze on the floor at a point about 60–90 centimetres in front of you. Now establish your centred position by raising your whole body slowly and quietly, moving it repeatedly to the left and to the right, forward and around, until you feel solidly based. Breathe through your nose, letting the air come to you by distending the diaphragm. Exhale slowly and completely, getting all the air out of your lungs. As you inhale slowly, count 'one'. See this 'one' in your mind. As you exhale see the 'one' going down, down, down into your solar plexus, which is located about 5 centimetres below your navel. With your next breath, as you inhale, see the number 'two' in your mind. This, too, sinks down into your solar plexus as you exhale, taking its place beside the 'one'. Continue until you reach 'ten', then recommence at 'one'. You may find the counting difficult as your mind wanders. If you lose count, just start again at 'one'. Do not worry about it. Simply keep bringing your mind back to the counting/breathing process, gently and firmly.

Eventually you will find that your mind seems to descend into your solar plexus, which becomes the centre of your being. You will find your concentration on the numbers becomes better and better as you continue your practice. Your attention will still wander, with extraneous thoughts drifting in and out of your mind, but it will become increasingly easy to concentrate on the counting of your breath. Make no attempt to keep 'alien' thoughts out. Instead, just keep your mind on the counting. You may take note of the thoughts as they come in, thinking of them as birds floating into the room of your mind. See them coming in one window, drifting through, and leaving through the other window. Do not try to push the 'alien' thoughts out of your mind. Simply transfer your attention from them back to your counting. Perhaps you may become anxious or uncomfortable. Quiet sitting and concentration do sometimes create such feelings, because the usual ways we have of avoiding discomfort are restricted. If you feel uncomfortable, just accept it. If you feel pleasant, accept that with the same indifference. As you become more practised in doing so, you will be able to be quiet in both body and mind, and to enter the silence.

During a particular session, many meditators find that, after a while, the concentration on the mantra, word or breathing, is replaced by a floating feeling. This is more than physical relaxation, involving a beautiful sense of mental release. In such a state, much subconscious material flows easily into our minds, providing penetrating insights of which the conscious mind has been unaware. Perhaps it may be even as Emerson said, that as we enter the meditative silence we are able to hear 'the whisper of the gods'.

Our subconscious thoughts may not attain such godlike status in the eyes of many people, but their power to provide solutions to many of life's problems is incontestable. In our normal existence moments of silence are rare. We fill our waking hours with constant activity, buffeted incessantly by noise and turmoil. The meditative silence permits us to leave this environment, to withdraw, so that we let go our tensions and allow our minds to run free. In *The Subliminal Consciousness*, Frederick Myers has defined genius as 'a mental constitution which allows man to draw readily into conscious life the products of unconscious thought'. Perhaps, through your use of meditation as a means of combating anxiety, you may also reap the benefit of increased intellectual capability.

One last word on meditation involves a process I would term 'active meditation' as opposed to the various techniques I have so far outlined. The latter are essentially passive in nature. The great virtue of active meditation is that it facilitates a mind shift away from worries to concentration on specific actions. For example when we sit down to drink a cup of coffee our thoughts are seldom on what we are actually doing. Usually we are thinking of the past or the future for we are unaccustomed to living in the present. With active meditation we concentrate exclusively on the action of drinking our coffee. We feel the warmth of the cup in our fingers, smell the aroma, savour the taste and feel the sensations in our throat as we swallow. We live fully the present moment, intensifying the awareness of our daily activities while we are actually engaged in them. As we become involved in this form of meditation, we can shut our minds to fear and anxiety, losing ourselves in the pleasure of feeling our muscles move as we walk, our faces tingle to the cold breath of wind, our noses quiver at the scent of jasmine. It can be a marvellous experience living intensely the present moment, though we often spoil it by the way we talk to ourselves.

SELF-TALK TO TURN OFF WORRY

Listen to the things you say to yourself. They are important because we act according to what we say. It is so easy to increase our fears by telling ourselves how catastrophic a situation is. You are carrying the dinner dishes into the kitchen prior to washing up, bump into a door and, in attempting to regain your balance, let go of your burden. As you survey the wreckage of the dishes, the reasonable reaction is something like 'Damn, what a nuisance', because that is what it is, a misfortune, not a tragedy. Yet, in such a situation, it is so easy to tell yourself how awful it is, how hopeless you are, and how fate is always against you. You tell yourself you are a born loser and nothing ever goes right. This is what I would describe as 'catastrophizing'. The more you go on in this vein, the more anxious and upset you make yourself. To what point? What pay-off is there for you? Why worry about the accident? It is over, and all your fretting will not help at all. It is such a little thing, yet so often it is these trivialities that upset us so badly. Perhaps there is some truth in the saying that we can dodge an elephant but we cannot dodge a fly. Confucious, in his wisdom, has said that men do not stumble over mountains but over molehills.

It is often necessary to talk to yourself in a rational way, telling yourself how you should cope with situations. This really involves identifying the specific situation that is proving troublesome and setting down on paper the ideas that you are actually telling yourself about it. In particular, look at the awful things which you are telling yourself are likely to happen as a result of the situation. Most of the time we do tend to 'catastrophize', exaggerating out of all proportion the actual seriousness of the problem we have. An old Swedish proverb says: 'Worry often gives a small thing a big shadow.'

After you list the ideas you are telling yourself, try to improve those which can be improved, and to then accept those which cannot. Part of the difficulty here is drawing this distinction between the things you can do something about and the things you cannot. Still, it is necessary to challenge the rather irrational sentences that you are telling yourself. Once you are able to do this, a problem which looms so large with such terrifying consequences often becomes easily manageable and far reduced in importance. This is largely a matter of co-operating with the inevitable.

If you know a circumstance is beyond your power to change or revise, say to yourself: 'It is so; it cannot be otherwise.' This has particular meaning for me as I write. None of us is perfect, fortunately, and I am no exception to the rule. Normally I can accept the inevitable without fretting about it but recently Hobart, my home city, has been experiencing its worst spell of spring and summer weather for fifty years — day after day of grey skies and drizzle. Obviously I cannot do anything about the weather — I have to accept it — yet I have been complaining and moaning about it, making myself thoroughly upset and unhappy. I adore the sun and my eagerly anticipated summer holiday was being ruined. I moped around aimlessly for days, until I decided I should return to writing this book. Once I did, I became engrossed to such an extent that when the fine weather came it was an intrusion. I worked out a compromise — some sun, some writing — but it brought home to me very forcibly that co-operating with the inevitable can bring rewards.

We can shut the door on our worries so that they cease to bother us by talking to ourselves. Mariko, the Japanese lover of the English navigator, Blackthorne, in James Clavell's *Shōgun*, tells us how to do this when she says to him:

Please, I implore you to be Japanese. Put this incident away — that's all it is, one incident in ten thousand. You must not allow it to wreck your harmony. Put it away into a compartment . . . Look at this rock. Listen to it growing . . . Put your mind on that . . . The stupidity of worrying about what it is . . . It is. So nothing can be done about it. A moment ago we were all almost dead. So all the worry and heartache was a waste, wasn't it?

Such a simple solution. You could do well to adopt such a philosophy. When you are caught up in the daily pressures of life, consider the things that are fretting you. Ask yourself: 'Is this matter really so urgent that if I stopped worrying about it and played golf or went shopping would there be catastrophic results?' If the answer is 'yes', obviously you have to do the task. Even a 'maybe' suggests you have something that needs doing. Doing, that is, not worrying. So often, though, the answer is 'no'. Things we worry about really do not matter at all, either to us or anyone else.

If, on the other hand, you are confronted with something really serious, self-talk can still help. Remind yourself that trouble is a tunnel through which we pass and not a brick wall against which we must break our heads. Everything passes.

When we lose someone we love dearly it seems as if our world has come to an end. It has not. Gradually we accept the loss and, if we are wise, continue to live each day as fully as possible. Grief passes. When deeply troubled, console yourself with the thought that 'this too will pass'.

The belief that every adversity carries within it the seed of an equivalent or greater benefit can be another comfort at such a time. I am sure the people of Hobart who lived on the eastern shore of the River Derwent did not think this way when the Tasman Bridge linking them with the city on the western shore was rammed by a ship and put out of action for three years. Normal transport patterns were basically disrupted. Though ferry services were greatly increased, eastern shore residents suffered considerable hardships in being cut off from the facilities of the city. The negative result was much misery and inconvenience, but the benefits were great. Road works and various forms of social services were provided within a space of three years which, under normal circumstances, would not have been completed for another twenty years. Instead of remaining dormitory areas, the eastern shore suburbs developed varied functions, providing a more satisfying environment for residents. When the bridge link was restored these gains were retained, so adversity had brought quite unanticipated benefits. No matter how dark your current situation, tell yourself that equal or greater benefits are there, ready to be revealed to you.

There are so many other things you can tell yourself whenever you feel worried and anxious. Throughout this book I have used quotations liberally, both to illustrate certain points I am making but also because they have been important to me in my own efforts to cope with anxiety. Hopefully, they will help you too, providing some support in facing your own problems. What I write is not theory, but is the fruit of my own experience. Like you, I know what it is to feel fear, to be anxious, to dwell on trivial worries that crowd my mind. I know that these saboteurs of our happiness can be controlled, can be overcome. Being able to tell yourself something positive to combat these negative emotions does work. When I am beset by problems which are affecting me negatively, the simple

'Everything passes', or 'Self-trust is the first secret of success have, on many occasions, helped me change the direction of my thinking. I use these two quotations only as examples for all those used in this book have proven valuable in one situation or another.

Have faith that you can talk yourself into calm confidence. After all, the antidote to fear is faith. Fear is really a form of negative belief while faith is a form of positive belief. Faith may take many forms. My basic theme throughout this book is for you to have faith in yourself, in the power you have to control your life through the thoughts you feed into your mind. Faith in God can also be a very powerful means of lifting you from unhappiness. William James always regarded prayer as the 'sovereign cure for worry'. Another great psychologist, Alfred Adler, saw the problem of every adult neurotic as 'that of finding a genuinely religious outlook on life'.

An almost inexhaustible mine of positive thoughts to help you cope with worry is provided by Dale Carnegie in *How to Stop Worrying and Start Living*. I feel this book provides easily understood and sensible guidance, helping people cope more successfully with life's problems. Comments such as 'Let the past bury its dead', 'What are the odds against this thing happening at all', and 'Count your blessings not your sorrows' may all be included, where appropriate, in the positive statements you make to yourself.

One Carnegie formula I think you will find of great benefit when faced with serious trouble is to ask yourself: 'What is the worst that can possibly happen?' Prepare yourself to accept this if you have to. Although this may initially provoke negative thoughts, you proceed to think of all the ways you can improve upon the worst. This more positive approach works against the earlier gloominess. In my experience it is very rare for the worst to ever happen, but by mentally preparing yourself, your spirits lift as things turn out to be not so bad after all. By organizing the facts pertinent to your problem you clarify the nature of your anxiety and this in itself is of great benefit.

This clarification can be even more effective if you systematically outline your problem, the source of your anxiety, on paper. Ask yourself these questions: 'What is the problem? What is its cause?' Then write down the answers as best you can. By so doing you make it easier for yourself to make a decision on the action you should take. Much of our anxiety is caused by indecision, so this you combat by the above method. Also it helps you act, and action is the enemy of anxiety which thrives on passivity and doubt. It was Bernard Shaw who said: 'The secret of being miserable is to have leisure to bother about whether you are happy or not.' The word 'miserable' could be replaced by 'anxious' without altering Shaw's basic truth. Keeping yourself busy is one of the best antidotes to anxiety. But when you are taking action, concentrate on the task you are doing, not upon yourself doing the task. Forget self and worries, lose yourself in doing something outside yourself and worry will find it very difficult to invade your mind.

5. Health & Healing

MENTAL HEALING

Self-help is the way to a better life. Within each of us lies the power to make our life what we want it to be. Nowhere is this so apparent as in the state of health we enjoy. Through the use of auto-suggestion and the maintenance of a positive mental attitude we can go far towards the prevention and cure of sickness. The fundamental principles of mind control outlined in chapter 3 apply very strongly in helping our bodies develop resistance to illness. Remember that the subconscious mind can exercise great control over the functioning of the body. Recall, too, that the subconscious mind, in turn, is under the influence of suggestions given by the conscious mind. It follows, then, that the functions of the body can be controlled by the conscious mind through the directions it issues.

John Barry suffered with bad headaches. He had done so for years and frequent medical treatment had been unable to help him. Repeatedly he had been told that his problem was due to 'nerves', to 'tension', and that the cure lay within himself. After John and I talked about his problem, he expressed a determination to do just that, to cure himself. He realized that he could treat his subconscious mind as if it was a separate entity capable of responding to the suggestions he gave it. His first suggestion was that his headache was about to cease; then that it was gradually becoming less severe until only mild discomfort was felt; and finally that it had ceased entirely. This gradual process is far more effective than commanding your headache to stop immediately.

John's suggestions were spoken aloud as he relaxed with eyes closed, although the same effect may have been achieved if he prefered to speak silently to himself. He persisted with the suggestions, repeating them quietly over and over again until the desired effect was produced. As he felt some improvement with the severe pain moderating to a milder discomfort, John's belief grew and his positive affirmations became more confident. He continued with suggestions of diminished severity, until his final decisive statement that the headache had gone completely. This was repeated a number of times until he was quite free of pain. Should some slight vestiges of discomfort remained, John would have ignored this, persisting in the suggestion that pain had ceased. By so doing he would have acted 'as-if' his goal had been achieved and, as we have seen earlier, this behaviour encourages a favourable outcome.

John followed his successful treatment by declarations that he was now free of headaches, that such symptoms were no longer part of him and would return. Due to his ever-increasing confidence in the power of his own mind, he was able to make such affirmations with considerable belief in their efficacy. Of course, success may not always be so instantaneous as it was with John, but persistence usually brings the desired result. Should he have desired to do so, he could have assisted the mental healing process by placing his hand on the area of discomfort. The warmth engendered by the hand contact could have been seen as a healing force easing away the pain.

VISUAL AND VERBAL SUGGESTION

Coupling the use of imagination with the spoken suggestion increases the power of the treatment. Recent research has indicated that many sufferers from severe migraine headache can gain relief by imagining certain processes taking place in their bodies. Suggestions are given that body metabolism will correct itself with health and strength increasing, and that the migraine sufferer will be able to control his symptom from this moment on. He will be able to do so by imagining, as soon as he senses the beginning of a migraine, that his right hand is becoming warm. Various mental images may be used to assist this feeling. Perhaps he imagines his heart pumping blood and vitality into his hand, he may visualize himself warming it in front of a fire or immersing it in warm water. Linked to this warm hand sensation is that of forehead coolness. Again the imagination helps. Mental images of a cool compress placed on the forehead or of gently rubbing the area with ice often prove very effective. The purpose of such visualization is to help the body draw blood from the affected area—the head—away to another area, in this case the hand. This permits the arteries in the head to control and combat the onset of migraine. Your visual and verbal instructions to the subconscious mind are able to effect these body changes.

This type of approach dates back to the work of Emile Coué, 'the father of auto-suggestion', and even earlier. He argued that whatever thought we continually hold in our minds, provided it is reasonable, tends to become an actual condition of our life. Therefore, thinking about an illness aggravates it. If we constantly think of health we become healthy. The important thing is to think of the end result. That is, if you have a headache, think of a head free from pain and your subconscious mind will accomplish it for you. In *Self-Mastery through Conscious Auto-Suggestion*, Coué incorporated all such specific suggestions in his general formula: 'Day by day, in every way, I'm getting better and better.' This was to be repeated twenty times when the subconscious mind is most accessible, particularly just before falling asleep at night. Such repetition was to be done quite effortlessly, letting the mind wander at will.

Coué warned against setting our faith a task greater than it can accomplish. A deaf person, for example, could hardly suggest 'I hear perfectly.' He also pointed out that it is inadvisable to mention the particular ailment or difficulty against which your suggestions are aimed. Following this advice, John Barry should not have talked about his headache, but concentrated on the opposite positive approach. His suggestions would have been that his head was feeling better and better, easier and easier, more and more comfortable, completely eliminating the mention of ache or pain.

I have certain reservations whether Coué's advice here is necessarily true, although I take his point that it is preferable to avoid naming negative conditions and to concentrate on their opposites. When you do so, avoid all words expressing doubt. It is not 'I hope my head will feel comfortable', but 'my head *will* feel more comfortable'. This desired improvement should not be thought of as taking place entirely in the future. Affirm that the change has already begun and that it will continue to operate with increasing rapidity until the end is fully attained.

There is a proviso I should like to make about this process of healing through suggestion. I think it advisable to place a limit on the time you will give yourself to effect a cure. This is not because I doubt the effectiveness of the treatment. I do not. I have used it so successfully myself and helped others do likewise that my belief is unshakable. However, it cannot cure or prevent *all* illness, only that which is mentally induced. Where there are organic malfunctions, medical help is essential though maintenance of a positive mental attitude is of great benefit in helping the body heal itself. Still, perhaps this proviso may not impose too great a restriction. Hans Selye, in his studies of stress in human beings, *Stress without Distress*, has claimed that approximately 75 per cent of patients visiting medical practitioners have no organic illness at all but are suffering from mentally induced illness. Many doctors confirm this figure, so it seems we have a wide field in which to practise the art of mental healing.

The hypochondriac, for example, constantly fills his mind with thoughts of sickness and illness. He concentrates on his own body, his own state of health, to such an extent that he virtually makes himself sick. This is quite easy to do, for at any particular time, if you concentrate upon your body, you are sure to find some part of it which aches, probably very mildly. By concentrating upon this area of slight discomfort, within twenty minutes or so you can make yourself feel so bad that you will take to your bed for the rest of the day. We are so suggestible.

I am reminded of an experiment I did with medical students while we were looking at ways of changing people's moods. Certain students were instructed to greet their fellows with very negative type comments when they met them at the day's first class. They would say things like: 'Had a bad night?' 'You look off-colour this morning.' 'Aren't you feeling well?' A second group said things like: 'You must have slept well.' 'You look really great this morning.' 'You must feel well, you look so fit.' After a week had elapsed, we interviewed the students who had been exposed to this treatment, explaining what had been going on. The effect of mind on physical health was clearly demonstrated. Students exposed to the negative comments on their state of health started feeling bad, no matter how well they had felt before coming to work. Many said they actually felt sick, as if they were coming down with something. On the other hand, those exposed to the positive comments felt good. Several said how their spirits lifted despite having arrived at university feeling off-colour and lethargic. Never underestimate the influence of your thoughts on your state of health.

DO NOT USE HEALTH TO EXCUSE FAILURE

It is easy, particularly if you are inclined to hypochondria, to use health as an excuse for failure. Evan Davies would tell anyone who cared to listen what a success he would have been in business if he had not been dogged by ill-health. As it was, he barely made both ends meet as owner of a small hardware shop. Yet, most of his illness was mentally induced and therefore under his own control. He improved dramatically once he forced himself to think more positively. For one thing, he refused to talk about his health. If you persist in talking about illness, it is akin to putting fertilizer on weeds. You also bore people. The old saying 'Smile and the world smiles with you, weep and you weep alone' sums up people's reactions rather well, I think. So Evan cut talk of ill-health out of his conversation.

He also concentrated on the parts of his body that were free from aches and pains, being grateful that he felt as healthy as he did. Nobody makes us concentrate on discomfort. We do this unaided. Accordingly, we have freedom to think about those parts of the body that feel good and revel in this experience. These simple changes in his thinking made a tremendous difference to Evan. Giving up ill-health as an excuse for failure, he channelled the energy previously used for complaining into generating new ideas for his business, which is now more prosperous. It does take a lot of energy to worry about something, such as the state of your health. On the other hand, smiling takes very little energy.

POSITIVE EXPECTANCY AND HEALING

Recent reports from England suggest that people entering hospitals for major surgery with a positive expectancy that the operation will be successful tend to recover more quickly and completely than do those entering with a negative expectation. This is part of the general pattern of how people choose to think about themselves and their health. When a person who is used to being healthy becomes ill, he tends to think it simply will not last, that he will soon be up and about again. Conversely, a person who is used to being sick tends to think, if he does have a period when he is feeling well, that it cannot possibly last. His negative expectancy virtually guarantees that this will be the case. He will soon revert to his normal feeling of ill-health, much of which is mentally induced. Of course there may be factors, other than the mental attitude, which are operating in such circumstances, but healers throughout the ages provide concrete evidence of the importance of positive expectation.

The results gained by such healers provide a lesson for us. I believe we all have healing powers, yet most of us never use them. Perhaps this is through ignorance of their existence or lack of confidence in ourselves. There is a parallel here with hypnosis. Folklore would have it that the hypnotist has strange, mysterious powers and that only a special sort of person is capable of exerting such influence. Yet this is not the case. It is really the subject or patient who has the power, for it is he who permits, or does not permit, himself to enter the trance state. Anyone can really help another person to enter a hypnotic trance. It is all a matter of having confidence in oneself and learning a few simple techniques. So it is with healing.

THE IMPORTANCE OF SELF-CONFIDENCE

Perhaps the *only* real obstacle to success experienced by the uninitiated healer is this lack of self-confidence. His education has normally dissuaded him from such endeavours, for mental healing is still considered a rather outlandish idea. In fact his education has probably been one of the chief culprits for his lack of belief in his own powers. Repeatedly we are taught, either explicitly or implicity, that our own intuitions, emotions and values are of little importance. Instead, there are always 'experts' who tell us how to do things, how to think, how to live our lives. It usually takes a long time for us to combat the negative aspects of our schooling, overriding them through the counter-suggestions we generate for ourselves. Some of us never manage to achieve this freedom from the constraints of an education so obsessed with conveying facts that it neglects to provide any really positive guidance on successfully living.

If the beginner persists, however, he will find it easier and easier to overcome the resistance of previous conditioning. As he realizes, perhaps faintly at first, the power to heal that he possesses, his conscious mind no longer raises obstacles but supports the truth of the suggestions. With both conscious and subconscious minds in harmony, the effect of his suggestions, whether directed towards the healing of someone else or of himself, is tremendously powerful. Sometimes instantaneous cures are the result. Belief in the efficacy of mental healing is necessary for its success and this is more readily generated when the conscious mind is able to let go of the negative prejudices of earlier educational experience.

Using the principles of mental healing you will be able not only to better cope with disease but, perhaps more importantly, to more effectively protect yourself against its occurrence. To do so, you must develop a highly positive attitude denying the power of disease to assert any mastery over you. Again, perfection here is unattainable because some sickness is organic in nature. None the less, at the first signs of approaching illness it is advisable to immediately start therapeutic auto-suggestion. This auto-suggestion can be profitably coupled with healing directed towards a sick friend. It seems a basic law of nature that through helping others we help ourselves. A most effective cure for worry is, in fact, to immerse yourself in somebody else's problem. As you concentrate your thoughts on helping the other person, you forget your own worries. When you return to them they usually seem so trivial that you let them go.

Mary Baker suffered violent attacks of hay-fever on a number of occasions every year. Allergy tests produced a variety of likely causes, but treatment based on these had proven ineffective. At the time Mary consulted me about her problem, her friend Angela had suffered a broken arm. This had not knitted well, and had to be broken and reset in hospital. Healing was progressing very slowly. I indicated to Mary that she might help her friend by directing healing thoughts to her before she fell asleep at night. For this is really all that mental therapy involves: it is based on the proposition that man has an inherent power enabling him to communicate his thoughts to others.

SUGGESTION AND PASSIVITY

The most favourable condition for the reception of such communication is one of perfect passivity, a state most readily attained during sleep. Therefore, to engage in mental healing the healer sends his message just before he falls asleep at night, anticipating that the recipient is probably asleep at this time. As Hudson, the author of *Psychic Phenomena*, puts it: 'The whole science of mental healing may be expressed in two words—passivity and suggestion.' He also maintains that best results are obtained when the patient is not informed beforehand of what is intended. The reason for this is that the patient cannot handicap the healer through adverse auto-suggestion at the subconscious level.

In addition to her healing of Angela, Mary used auto-suggestion to combat her own hay-fever. She was completely successful in this latter endeavour, and has not had an attack in over a year. As far as her attempt to heal Angela is concerned, it is impossible to estimate her effectiveness. Her friend's recovery was quite rapid, rather more so than her doctor expected.

What Mary attempted was absent healing, a type often taking place in church groups which come together for this very purpose. The theory is that a group of people united by a single aim can generate more power than they can operating as separate individuals. A chair, representing the absent patient, is placed in the centre of the group which is in a circle. Alternatively, one member of the healing circle may occupy the chair, acting as a proxy for the patient. The absent person is visualized in the chair and healing energy directed towards her, either in a generalized way or specifically to the afflicted part of the body. Perhaps she can be seen as surrounded by white light, which gradually thickens until her image disappears. A few seconds are allowed to pass and the patient is seen emerging as if from a fog, completely healed. Usually participants are in a relaxed, meditative state as they direct their healing powers in this way.

When the afflicted person is actually present, healing may proceed in the same way or, alternatively, physical contact, the 'laying on of hands', may be used. Some healers believe they are instruments of an outside force, that they serve only as a mediator channelling healing energy from this power to the sufferer. The same belief is held by many who practise self-healing. They imagine themselves surrounded by healing energy, perhaps visualized as white light. This is allowed to penetrate so that the whole body seems to vibrate with its force. The healing energy is breathed in, being specifically directed to the third eye position in the centre of the forehead, the throat, the heart, the solar plexus (located 5 centimetres below the navel), the base of the spine and the crown of the head in that order. Usually when power is directed to the heart, the arms tingle and the fingertips pulsate. This is the time to lay the fingertips on the afflicted part of the body. Believers in this particular approach term it psychic healing. If you are interested in learning more about the specific techniques for harnessing the energy of the universe for the purpose of healing, I suggest you read Joseph Wead's books, *The Wisdom Of The Mystic Masters* and *Psychic Energy*.

Whatever label we use, be it psychic healing or mental therapeutics, the fact remains that we do have great power to heal both ourselves and other people if we will only permit ourselves to do so. Basically it appears that the body, given proper circumstances and environment, will heal itself. It seems that we have a most efficient regulatory system within us that normally keeps our bodies in excellent working order as long as we simply keep out of its way. We can do this by believing with complete conviction that good health is our natural state, and refusing to think about our ailments, be they real or imaginary.

RELAXATION PROMOTES HEALTH

Let us assume now that you accept the importance of a positive mental attitude as the key to good health. There are other things you can do to maintain this condition. As has been pointed out above, relaxation is of great value. Throughout the day take short five-minute breaks in which you let go various muscle groups. Of particular importance are the forehead, the jaw, the stomach and the hands. Concentrate on first tightening then relaxing these muscles and your whole body will feel at ease. Then briefly use mental images of pleasant scenes, places where you feel at peace and imagine you are there. If you do this your working day will seem so much easier. Because you are releasing all that energy tied up in keeping yourself tense, you will find you are doing things effortlessly, without strain.

Check on yourself as you work, particularly if yours is a sedentary job. Are your legs tense? Do your shoulders and the back of your neck feel tight? Is your jaw clamped firmly shut? They do not have to be. Such tension does not help you work any better. It makes life more difficult. Mentally check on your body, letting go the tightness until this becomes a habit. Keep your body easy and relaxed, so that only the muscles actually being used are tense. Adopt a little Zen philosophy, realizing that the harder you strive the less likely you are to achieve your objective. Like all concepts this can be overdone so we remain in complete passivity but, in moderation, it is a wise injunction. Let go and let things happen rather than trying to force them to happen. Often we are so busy rushing to achieve some goal that we overlook the enjoyment we can get along the way. According to Zen philosophy it is the journey that is important, not the destination, so relax and enjoy your work. It seems that using our will-power, forcing ourselves to strive, often achieves nothing. It may even have the opposite effect.

I am reminded here of Tony Graham, a hard-driving business executive, who is an old friend of mine. Tony worries continually that he is falling behind in all the things he thinks he should do. He frets continually if delayed by traffic or if he has to wait for an elevator. He feels he is on a treadmill, frantically striving to obtain the best of material things for his family, fine home, prestige car, expensive clothes. So hard does he drive himself that he has no time for anything else but work. His family see little of him. He is always running. Not surprisingly, among other things Tony developed high blood pressure. Now striving to make your blood pressure return to normal just does not work. You can not force it down. If you try, you are more likely to aggravate the condition. You are far more likely to succeed by wishing your blood pressure to go down in a quiet, passive way and then simply allowing it to happen. The secret lies in the control of passive energy through a kind of meditative approach.

It took some time to convince Tony that he could take time each day to relax and let go; to meditate and forget his striving for a while. It also was not easy for him to learn how to enter the meditative silence, to be passive and let things happen. Yet he did learn to do so. Within three months his blood pressure had returned to normal and his general health was vastly improved. The additional bonus lay in his increased efficiency as an executive. Working less hours, taking time off for relaxation, walking instead of running should, in his previous view, have led to a drastic decline in his income-earning power. When this did not happen and his value to his firm increased instead of declined, Tony was confirmed in a changed life-style. His family, too, was delighted for he now spent more time with them.

Tony, like so many other people, also discovered the benefits of napping. Short naps of ten or twenty minutes, particularly around the middle of the day, can be enormously refreshing. Some experimentation is necessary to find the best length of time for you so you awake refreshed, ready to start the day anew. Have no fear about sleeping too long. All of us have an unconscious sense of time which works whether we are asleep or awake. Just before dropping off, visualize a clock or watch showing the time you wish to end your nap, and tell yourself you will awaken then. These short naps can often be as restful as many hours in bed because it is the actual process of falling asleep that embodies much of the benefit. In fact, simply relaxing deeply for ten to twenty minutes is a great help in revitalizing the system.

I would not, however, like you to believe that I think everyone should lie down and spend most of their lives sleeping or relaxing. It is just that normally we are so busy, so anxious, so harried, that we allow ourselves too little time to 'just let go'. What I am suggesting is that relaxation is so beneficial it is well worth your while to deliberately make available some time each day, say ten to twenty minutes, to practise the techniques I have outlined. You will feel more energetic and, as a result, your work and life will flow more easily.

INCREASING YOUR ENERGY

There are many other ways of increasing your energy too. Resting overmuch should be countered by forcing yourself to do something productive every day, so that you keep momentum. Muscles and thoughts seem to become very sluggish unless stimulated in this way. Writing a book provides a good example. I attempted to write this book in fits and starts but found, if I let it go for week or so, it was difficult to start again. I was unhappy with what I had written so scrapped it and started again over my summer vacation. I set myself the task of writing for three hours every day. Once this pattern was established the work flowed quickly and I enjoyed it immensely. So, if you want your energy to flow, keep active each day, preferably through doing things you like. Do not just think about it, for then you only worry about things which need to be done. Do them now and avoid the tiredness engendered by such worry.

Tiredness so often comes from boredom, too. Combat this and find new energy by setting up a goal, or a number of goals, at which to aim. This channels your thinking purposefully, and energy comes from your thoughts. The person with a goal, with things to do, never lacks energy because of this sense of purpose. It is the drifter, seeing no point in his existence, who seems to be perpetually tired. He lacks enthusiasm, which is probably the greatest generator of energy that exists. As Samual Ullman put it: 'Years wrinkle the skin but to give up enthusiasm wrinkles the soul.'

Yes, energy or its lack is intimately connected with your thoughts. Optimism, the will to succeed, makes us tingle with zest, for the mind can either generate energy for you or drain it off in accordance with what you think. Bill Jones seemed to be chronically fatigued. He achieved this undesirable state through the burden of guilt he carried. His small son drowned in the back-yard swimming-pool while Bill was away from home. He had been enjoying a Sunday barbecue with his family when his services as a medical practitioner were required at the local hospital. It was after he had attended to his patient that he heard of his family tragedy. 'If I had been home, it might never have happened. I might have saved him', ran Bill's thoughts, a recurrent theme that still occupied his mind two years after the drowning. He brooded constantly.

It is true Bill may have prevented the tragedy, but there was no certainty of this. His wife, a trained nurse, was there. So, too, were Bill's other children, both older than the drowned victim and both strong swimmers with a knowledge of life-saving techniques. Blaming himself and feeling guilty Bill became very depressed and lethargic, of little use either to himself or to anyone else. This is the attitude he chose to take. Perhaps a healthier one would have been to reflect on how much he had done for his son while he was alive, for he had been an excellent father to the boy. Negative feelings had drained away his energy, seriously impairing the help he could give his patients and his family. To me this seems a bad bargain.

THE IMPORTANCE OF EXERCISE

Most of this chapter has been concerned with the mind and its role in health. Perhaps it is now appropriate for at least a brief look at something more physical, such as the part played by exercise. Many of us play a leisurely game of golf once a week and feel we have fulfilled our obligations in this direction. Others sit quietly at a desk all week and spend one hour flinging ourselves madly around a squash court. This behaviour, far from promoting health, invites disaster, as the numerous heart attacks occurring in such situations would indicate. Studies conducted by US National Aeronautics and Space Administration scientists confirm that exercise every day is desirable. If this is impossible, the minimum requirement is three non-consecutive days each week. This is because unexercised muscles deteriorate very quickly, being unable to store 'conditioning'. On reading this, many people will say: 'I simply haven't the time to go off and play squash, tennis, or golf three times a week.' True, but exercise does not *have* to be of this sort.

Walking is perhaps the best all-round body conditioner there is. However, idly ambling along, stopping to pick daisies or looking into shop windows, does not qualify as walking. The pace should be brisk so that perhaps striding is a better description of this aid to your health. Each of us has a natural stride, and dropping into it several times a day promotes a feeling of well-being. A popular remedy for anger is to walk it off, for striding improves the disposition. It also improves blood circulation and oxygen intake, thus providing beneficial exercise for the heart. Thus a steady diet of striding, utilizing virtually all the body's muscles as it does, builds up resistance to fatigue. Perhaps its greatest advantage is that it can be incorporated into your normal schedule of daily living.

Herein, I think, lies the secret of successful exercise. Rather than seeing it as something apart that has to be scheduled separately, make it part of your life-style. Use the car less and walk more. Avoid lifts and walk up and down stairs. If you travel to work by bus, get off a stop or two before your destination and briskly walk the rest of the way. It takes little time but the rewards are great, not the least being the tranquillizing effect. Evidence derived from research into the effect of exercise on retired people indicates that a fifteen-minute walk reduces neuromuscular tension more effectively than 400 milligrams of tranquillizer.

The benefits of walking can be enhanced by the meditative concentration described in chapter 4. Feel your muscles working, experience the glow of well-being, revel in the zest of your step, and continually dwell on the way this pleasurable activity is improving your health. Such concentrated awareness heightens the sensations of the moment, bringing mind and body together in a harmony promoting good health.

COPING WITH OVERWEIGHT

Mind and body come together in another approach to improved health, too. Of all the many threats to our physical well-being, obesity is one of the most dangerous. Insurance companies make calculations on life expectancies to guide the size of the premiums they charge. A person aged forty-five who carries as little as 4.5 excess kilos increases his chances of dying prematurely by 8 per cent. If this excess climbs to 10 kilos, he has a 20 per cent greater chance of early death than a person of the same age whose weight is normal. Not only does life expectancy decrease with overweight, so too does the general level of health. The obese person carries around a heavy burden, tiring himself more than his lighter brethren. Hot weather often engenders a chronic fatigue which saps his will to do things. A chain reaction sets in because, as I have indicated above, it is this desire for activity that generates fresh energy. The more we do, the more we seem able to do. So the over-weight person loses out all ways.

Accepting that obesity is an important problem is one thing. Doing something about it is something else again. Magazines abound with articles telling you how to lose weight, setting out one diet after another. Books on diet flood the market. Health clinics promote courses ranging from the simple to the complex, while weight-watchers clubs have mushroomed throughout the Western world. Obviously people are interested, wanting help. Perhaps too often they expect someone else to solve their problems for them. They search for the magic method which will effortlessly enable the fat to melt away, never to return. Life is not really so accommodating. An old saying is that God helps those who help themselves. If you are prepared to help yourself you can lose weight and stabilize at the level you wish to. After all, that is the real issue. Actually losing weight is possible on almost any kind of diet. The trick is to keep it off. Studies conducted at hospital out-patient clinics suggest that less than 5 per cent of people are able to maintain their desired weight once they have attained it.

Conventionally, the answer to overweight has been calorie counting. It makes sense that if you eat fewer calories each day you must lose weight. In theory this may be true, yet because people metabolize food at different rates, your calories may not have the same results as the next person's. As Dr David Reuben has pointed out in *The Save-Your-Life Diet*, it is ironic that while millions of dieters struggle to save 20 calories here or cut carbohydrates to 30 grams a day, millions of other people, rural Africans, for example, consume 3000 calories daily and 600 grams of carbohydrate without gaining any weight at all. The resolution of this apparent paradox seems to lie in the type of food eaten rather than the calorie content. Obese people tend to live on a low-roughage diet high in refined sugar and ultra-refined white flour products. Dr Reuben suggests that such a diet is so appetising that it virtually compels over-eating. Further, because the obese person tends to eat quickly, he consumes great quantities of food before he feels satisfied. The delay between actually eating enough food to satisfy you and indication from your appetite-control centre that this has occurred, is sufficient to permit the intake of much unnecessary additional food. This delay seems to be greater for obese people than for those with normal appetites.

The moral seems clear. To lose weight, slow down your rate of eating. By so doing, you will satisfy your appetite with less food. In fact, this slowing down process may be coupled with the active meditation described above. It is a matter of focusing your intense awareness upon each mouthful of food. Adam Smith, in *Powers Of Mind*, puts it this way:

With each bite you go: Reaching, reaching. Lifting, lifting. Taking, taking. Chewing, chewing. Tasting, tasting. Savouring, savouring. Swallowing, swallowing. Digesting, digesting . . . You always get a signal at each meal that says, that's almost enough, that's enough. You can move the signal forward in time by paying attention.

So the speed at which you eat is important. So, too, is what you choose to eat.

Dr Reuben's answer to the obesity problem lies in a high-roughage diet. The main elements are:

1 *The eating of:*

a. High-roughage foods, including whole-grain cereal products, high-fibre fruits and vegetables, and nuts and seeds wherever possible. Eat only fresh fruit and vegetables, raw if possible or with a minimum of cooking, keeping seeds, strings and skins intact.

b. Flour products made from whole-grain rye flour, whole-wheat flour, soy flour, whole-ground cornmeal, buckwheat flour (whole-grain) or carob flour without adding refined sugar and with a minimum of shortening.

c. Moderate amounts of low-fat meat, fish and poultry.

d. Moderate amounts of milk products. Also be moderate in use of fats and oils for cooking and salads.

e. Two teaspoonfuls of unprocessed miller's bran with a glass of water before each meal.

f. Two tablespoons of yoghurt daily.

2 *The drinking of:*

at least eight glasses of water a day.

3 *The elimination of:*

a. All low-roughage foods, all ultra-processed flour products and all refined sugar (including brown sugar). Molasses and honey can be used as substitutes.

b. All 'synthetic' or imitation products such as non-dairy creamers and artificial sour cream.

c. High-sugar, high-starch items such as ice-cream, sweets, soft-drinks, 'commercial' baked goods and pre-sweetened cereals.

d. Alcoholic beverages, because alcohol is so quickly converted to sugar in the body.

Perhaps such a drastic change in your eating habits is unappealing. It may also be unnecessary. Laurence Moorhouse, the co-author of *Total Fitness in Thirty Minutes a Week*, certainly thinks so. He warns against any form of drastic dieting which eliminates a particular type of food. Rather, his formula for permanent weight loss is to diminish daily food intake by 200 calories and to burn up 300 extra calories in physical activities. This 'reduction' of 500 calories per day results in a weight loss of half a kilo per week. Such a concept is very appealing, for the only 'dieting' involved is eliminating an extra slice of bread during the day. To burn off the 300 calories, Moorhouse suggests walking, jogging and various other activities of a similar nature.

However, all that may really be necessary is to do your daily tasks more energetically. As mentioned above, walking instead of taking the car, and climbing stairs instead of riding in lifts, is beneficial in this way. The same principle can be applied in many small ways. Standing consumes more calories than sitting, so it will contribute to your weight loss if you stay on your feet when talking on the phone or doing the ironing. Similarly, moving about requires more energy than sitting or standing still, so it is useful to 'pace' when thinking through a problem. Break up your periods of sitting by stretching, standing and walking around your home or office. Substitute your own power for that of machines by beating cream by hand, using a hand-saw instead of a power-saw. Engage in hobbies which require bending and stretching, such as gardening or, perhaps, simply clean and polish your car more often. It is simply a matter of using your body instead of allowing it to remain idle. As you do work your muscles, so you burn up calories and lose weight.

Half a kilo a week may not seem very much until you realize that is 26 kilos in a year. Losing that much weight over a period of a year, and keeping it off, is something most strict dieters would never achieve. Due to the deprivation of particular food and the effort of self-denial, strict dieters are prone to periodic lapses, eating all that is forbidden. Of course the weight goes back on. Feeling guilty, they embark again on the diet. Like a yo-yo, the weight goes up and down, a rather unhealthy state of affairs. With the gradual loss of half a kilo per week the weight just slips away, the body stabilizing itself at an ever-lower level.

To help you maintain such a re-orientation of your eating habits, the mind can be very valuable. Using the techniques of suggestion and imagination outlined above, visualize yourself standing on a set of scales showing the weight you would like to be. 'See' yourself looking the way you want to look when you are that weight. Imagine this very vividly last thing at night, immediately after waking in the morning, during your relaxation period and before meals. As you do, tell yourself you will enjoy the high-roughage foods you are eating. They will satisfy you completely and you will feel happy as you eat, knowing you are improving your health as you reduce your weight. For you will reap the benefits of reducing the likelihood of developing heart disease, diabetes and high blood pressure. In addition, tell yourself you will have absolutely no need or desire for low-roughage, high-sugar, high-starch foods and alcoholic drinks. In this way you condition your mind to enjoy the food that is good for you, and feel no need for that which causes your obesity. As you do, mind and body co-operate to improve your life through improving your health.

6. Improving Your Efficiency

THE EFFICIENT USE OF TIME

The amount of time at our disposal is limited. There are just so many hours in a day. If we are to assume control over our lives, then the way we use the time available to us is very important. The question of priorities and goals must be considered seriously, or you will find yourself drifting aimlessly, doing the things other people think you should do rather than those which feel right for you. As the American poet, Carl Sandburg, put it: 'Time is the coin of your life. It is the only coin you have, and only you can determine how it will be spent. Be careful lest you let other people spend it for you.'

Whenever I think of these words I wonder just how many of us realize the value of time. It is so precious, so irreplaceable, yet we fritter it away as if we were tapping some inexhaustible reservoir. Once we do realize its importance we can take steps to use time wisely so that we maximize our chances of achieving the things we wish to achieve. After all, the purpose of using time efficiently is not to make you work harder and longer. Rather, it is to enable you to do things more quickly, less wastefully, so that you have more leisure time. Once you create this extra time it is your choice how you will use it. Perhaps you will choose to work harder. Fine, if that is what you want. Perhaps you will spend it dozing in the sun. That is all right too. By using time efficiently you can give yourself more opportunity to live your life the way you want to.

Alan Lakein, in his excellent book, *How To Get Control Of Your Time And Your Life*, stresses that: 'Making the right choices about how you'll use your time is more important than doing efficiently whatever job happens to be around.' Knowing where you are going is of greater value to you than getting there quickly, yet so often we confuse activity with achievement. Herein lies the reason for so much 'busy work'. If we keep busy, even if it is with trivia, we feel we are doing something.

In his book *Getting Things Done*, Bliss divides our use of time into five categories:

- doing tasks which are both important and urgent.
- doing tasks which are important but not urgent.
- doing tasks which are urgent but not important.
- busy work which is marginally worth doing, but is neither important nor urgent.
- wasting time, which brings no sense of satisfaction or accomplishment after the time has been spent.

He argues that the effective individual is he who allocates more time to the 'important but not urgent' category. The ineffective person, on the other hand, never gets around to these 'important but not urgent' tasks because he spends too much time on the 'urgent but not important' and 'busy work' categories. Because he chooses to act in this way, he never finds time to take the exercise he feels he should, to visit the foreign countries which appeal to him, or to read the books which could broaden his viewpoint. Although these things might be important to the particular person involved, they get pushed down the priority scale by trivialities which seem to demand instant attention. In this way we let time use us. To assert more control over time, we need to plan our activities carefully so that we can achieve the things we want to achieve. Sitting quietly, thinking out new directions, meditating on our goals and ways to achieve them, is often seen as wasting time. Yet such planning is essential if we are to use time efficiently.

This emphasis on planning may seem a contradiction to the Zen philosophy of enjoying the journey, but it is not really so. Journeys can still be rewarding even if we are aware of a destination we wish to reach. Even the most pleasant of travels can lose its appeal quickly if it is completely aimless, so planning may add to enjoyment, rather than detracting from it.

MAKING LISTS AND SETTING PRIORITIES

The really important aspect of planning, as Lakein points out, involves making a list and setting priorities. In establishing these, categorize as A those items yielding the greatest return for your time, and as C those items which take considerable time for little result. B comes somewhere between the two. The criteria for making such a categorization relates to your goals. By asking yourself the question: 'What do I really want from life?' you can soon draw up a list of priorities. Subsidiary questions such as: 'What are my lifetime goals? How would I like to spend the next three years? If I had only six more months to live, how would I spend them?' will help you achieve this. From time to time your goals will change, so it is important to go through this exercise on a number of occasions each year.

There are other ways of looking at goals. Alexander Terrill, an acquaintance of mine, uses a listing procedure. First, at the beginning of each year he lists what he wants, those things he desires to get or achieve. Second, he takes a hard look at himself, noting down his limitations. These may include constraints on his time, family responsibilities, personality characteristics and financial limitations. Honesty and a sense of reality are very helpful in constructing this second list. Third, Alexander lists those items from his first list, his wants, which he feels he can get in the coming year, considering the limitations upon him. Thus, he draws up a rather flexible blueprint for his year, a series of targets which give his life a sense of direction. He knows how he intends to use his time, to advance himself towards the achievement of his goals. As with Lakein's approach, Alexander's goal-setting is the first step. Next come the actual mechanics.

The process of planning now goes into more detail. Having established what you want to achieve, it is helpful to take each goal, in order of priority, and decide all the possible activities which will assist in its realization. Again, set priorities to allow you to select the most productive activity to do at any given moment.

In brief, then, the essential steps in planning to use your time efficiently are listing possible long-term goals, setting priorities for now, thus identifying your most important A goals, listing possible activities by which these A goals can be achieved, setting priorities and identifying A activities for now, scheduling these activities, taking action and doing them as scheduled. Listing and setting priorities is the heart of the process, enabling you to use your time so you move forward towards the achievement of your goals. Scheduling is vital, too.

Here is where the process involves your day-to-day activities. A man I admired greatly in my youth was John Chalmers, a university lecturer. He was unfailingly helpful, seemed to have plenty of time to talk to his students, and was enthusiastically involved in several demanding hobbies and sports. Yet his lectures were very carefully prepared, he wrote many articles each year, and produced a book every two or three years. This may sound a little dull, but he was a man who really enjoyed life. Students liked him, his lectures were fun, and his colleagues admired his scholarship. I now realize that people like John Chalmers are relatively rare in any walk of life, not only in the academic world, which was the environment in which we met.

Through talking with John and people like him, whether they work in universities, the professions or businesses, I have realized that much of their success is due to the way they plan their activities, not only on the long-term basis outlined earlier in this chapter, but also on a day-to-day basis. When they start each day, they know what they are going to do, what they want to achieve. Most of them have this set down on paper as a list of things to do. These are arranged in order of priority and are crossed off as completed. This action in itself is very satisfying, for as you draw a line through an item it represents the achievement of a short-term goal, generating a feeling of accomplishment. When, at day's end, you have been able to cross off every item on your list, you feel really good, knowing you have made progress towards the important goals you have set yourself.

Even if you have not completed everything, you can feel content that you have used your time to best advantage, spending it on the A priority items instead of frittering it away aimlessly on low-priority C items. This is expressed neatly by Lakein's (*How to Get Control of Your Time and Your Life*) 80/20 rule. 'If all items are arranged in order of value, 80 per cent of the value would come from only 20 per cent of the items.' Many of these latter 80 per cent really do not need doing at all. Ask yourself what terrible things would happen if you did not do a particular C item. If you cannot think of any there is not much point in doing it when there are other more productive things to do.

GETTING THINGS DONE

The value of establishing daily schedules is that it encourages you to do things, to take action. We say things like 'I'll get around to it one of these days' but, of course, one of these days really means 'none of these days'. Pablo Picasso has made this point even more strongly in his statement: 'Put off until tomorrow only what you are willing to die having left undone.' Many of us will claim we just have not the time to do things, yet it is amazing how we can always find time to do those tasks which are really important to us. It is a matter of organizing our time effectively.

Arnold Bennett, the English writer, was one who did this superbly well. The last entry in his diary for 1929 reads: 'This year I have written 304,000 words: one play, two films, one small book on religion, and about eighty or eighty-one articles. Also I lost a full month in rehearsals and a full month, no, six weeks, on holidays.' In addition to his writing activities, Bennett enjoyed English social life to the full. He was, in fact, a man who accomplished a tremendous amount every year. What was his secret? He has set it out for us in his little book, *How to Live on Twenty-four Hours a Day*. Bennett felt that our main mistake lay in looking on the time spent at our work as 'the day' and the time spent before and after our working day as unimportant. Adoption of such an attitude killed interest in those hours and led to their waste. The solution he proposed was to arrange a day within a day, beginning after work and ending when the working day started. The evening was to be arranged so that it was not cut in half by the evening meal, thus a clear expanse of three hours was to be created. Bennett suggested that every second night, one and a half hours of this period be used in some important cultivation of the mind. In the words Bliss used (see p. 76 above), tasks which are important but not urgent could be accomplished during this time. The other nights were to be left free, but the thrice-weekly ninety-minute periods were to be kept sacred, so that nothing could interfere with them.

The time spent between leaving the front door and arriving at work could also be put to good effect, according to Bennett. In chapter 4 I mentioned his idea of deliberately training the mind to concentrate on one idea for a half-hour period each day: the 'travel-to-work' time was when Bennett suggested this could be accomplished.

ESTABLISHING DAILY SCHEDULES

Having specific tasks, organized in order of priorities, provides a series of targets. This helps you to start without procrastinating while you wait for conditions to be just right. A writer I know, who sets himself a target of a certain number of pages a day, sits at his desk each morning and if the ideas are not flowing writes his name over and over again, doodles and draws funny faces until he flows naturally into his assigned task. He is going through the mechanical motions of writing, instead of waiting for inspiration to occur. When we wait on something to happen, we are postponing action. It takes more effort to start a job than it does to keep at it once it has started. Approach your task by deciding what you are going to do and how you are going to do it, then start immediately. Your ideas alone will not bring you success – you have to act upon them.

One form of useful action to take is talking over ideas with other people, keeping yourself receptive and open. Extend yourself by mixing with vital, enthusiastic people who generate different approaches to problems, who advocate different ways of doing things. Do a lot of asking and listening, encouraging other people to talk. It is only when we allow others to comment on their own ideas and those we have put forward that we learn. The Bible says: 'He who hath knowledge spareth his words' [Proverbs 17.27]. In most gatherings you will find it is from the person who says relatively little that you can learn most. The individual who talks a great deal, dominating the conversation frequently, has little of real value to contribute. After all, as Epictetus put it: 'Nature has given men one tongue, but two ears, that we may hear from others twice as much as we speak.' This is not a bad policy to follow if you want to learn from other people.

HANDLING YOUR GRIEVANCES

However, in many person-to-person situations, the issues which arise are often not so much oriented towards learning but towards settling grievances between the two parties in ways that are relatively satisfactory to both. In *Help Yourself* John Lembo suggests a process of rational self-counselling as a means of coping with such situations. He points out that there are a number of useful steps you can take when lodging a grievance with someone else.

The most important of these are, first, to state your grievance as soon as you can express it clearly. At the same time, indicate how pleased you are with many other aspects of the other person's behaviour. This is the sandwich method of offering criticism – insert it between two layers of honest compliments.

Second, use 'I don't like it' type statements with the emphasis on 'I' rather than 'You are 'statements. When you say, for example, 'I don't like to be disappointed' you are describing your own feelings, taking responsibility for them. When you say 'You are inconsiderate' you are blaming the other person for causing your unhappiness. He may have something to do with it, of course, but *your* own attitudes and the way *you* think are very important, too. It is rare that grievances are generated by only one member of a couple.

Third, avoid dredging up the past. We are so good at this. When we present our grievances, they can trigger off so much negative emotion that we bring up all the complaints of the past whether they have anything to do with the current problem or not. This only aggravates the situation further, so focus on one complaint at a time.

Fourth, in a non-angry and non-demanding way, propose some realistic ways that the problem could be satisfactorily resolved. Try to arrive at a specific agreement about the *best* way of handling it.

It is unlikely that you will arrive at this best way of handling the grievance if you insist on blaming the other party. By blaming someone else, you avoid taking responsibility for yourself. It is all his or her fault. If only he or she was different, perhaps more like me, we would not have this problem. Thinking this way is fatal to the resolution of conflict. If we really want to settle grievances effectively, we have to give others the freedom to be themselves, to be different from us. Instead of interfering with other people it is likely to be more profitable for us to work on our own thoughts and attitudes.

To help you do so, Arnold Bennett, to whom I have referred on p. 79, has suggested you look upon yourself as a free agent, capable of change and flexibility. You are fortunate in being this way, but others may not be so blessed. They can be seen as the puppets of determinism, moulded by their environments to behave in the ways they do. They cannot help doing the things which annoy you, therefore it is rather pointless becoming upset by their actions and indulging in blame and criticism. By adopting such an attitude you avoid the temptation of interfering with them, attempting to change them in ways you think of as desirable. So whenever you are thwarted and frustrated by someone else, realize he is what he is and you cannot do anything about it.

Changing your own attitude in this way is, strangely enough, often instrumental in changing those of the people around you. As you give up blaming others, you will find you feel calmer, more cheerful, unjudgemental. Behaving in this way you will tend to create a more relaxed atmosphere, one in which it is easier for the other person to be reasonable and positive in resolving grievances. Confrontation engendered by blaming and criticizing gives way to co-operation based on avoidance of blame. Even if the other person involved in the grievance situation insists on being critical, you can turn this off by the method outlined above (p. 44), that of cheerfully agreeing with the criticism. It takes two to argue and once you refuse to play that game, grievance solution becomes far easier.

However, presenting the grievance to the other person in a way likely to lead to a successful outcome is only part of the process. Receiving a grievance from someone in a positive way is the other part. Show the other person you are giving him your full attention. Look directly at him, listen carefully and encourage him to speak. Accept the grievance as something of importance to the other person without accusing him of being irrational, defensive or insensitive. Realize that it is your behaviour that is at issue, so do not imply the other person has some sinister motive in lodging the grievance. Ask for the opportunity to reply. Re-state the grievance in your own words, thus showing you have been listening, and defend your actions if you honestly believe your behaviour was justified. Otherwise, admit you were wrong.

That is the hard part, of course. Admitting you were wrong. This is something all of us find very difficult to do. Strange, really, because what we are saying by such behaviour is: 'I'm perfect. I don't make mistakes. Therefore, I should never admit I've done anything wrong.' Hardly anyone believes this. Through membership of the human race we constantly make mistakes, bumble, do stupid things. So much unhappiness is caused, though, by acting as if we expected perfection from ourselves, and from others. Once you can accept yourself as a fallible human being, life becomes much easier. Do the same with other people, too. Instead of expecting perfection and feeling disappointed when you discover inevitable flaws, look for positive things to like about the people you meet. Everyone is a mixture of likeable and unlikeable attributes. It is really up to you upon which you concentrate. This opens up the whole question of interpersonal relationships which we shall now consider.

EFFICIENCY IN
INTERPERSONAL RELATIONSHIPS

Efficiency is probably an unusual word to use in this context. However, there are ways of doing things which facilitate friendship and closeness, and other ways which distance you from people. Assuming that most people prefer to have friends and acquaintances rather than to have none, I think behaviour that increases this likelihood could be described as efficient and that which decreases it as inefficient.

In its simplest form, efficiency in interpersonal relationships is really a matter of acting in ways that encourage people to like you. If you do something to or for someone that makes him feel good, he is likely to reciprocate. This is rewarding and you are likely to continue acting in the same way. You, in turn, reinforce the other person's behaviour so that a pleasant relationship may develop. It all seems to be a matter of reward. We tend to avoid people who leave us feeling neutral or negative, so have no opportunity to build a relationship with them. Conversely, people who rouse a positive response in us encourage further approach behaviour and a mutually rewarding interaction can develop, leading to friendship. Friendships develop through constant contact as soon as this is enjoyed by both parties. The issue, then, is how can you behave in ways that will help this situation to develop.

Recently I was at a party when I was introduced to Don Levitt. He was a very easy person to talk to. Afterwards, I realized that he had been the only person at the party with whom I had really enjoyed conversing. Virtually all my other interactions consisted of pleasantries about the weather, sport or work. Why had Don Levitt stood out so markedly? He was not outstandingly vivacious or dynamic. In fact, I thought of him as being very placid. Then it came to me. I realized that he had made me feel important, encouraging me to talk in terms of my own interests. Don seemed fascinated by my work with university staff, my use of hypnosis in therapy and my ideas on physical fitness. Though saying little himself, he seemed genuinely interested in me as a person. He was an excellent listener, his face smilingly attentive. It is very flattering for anyone, of course, to feel that someone is hanging on your every word. He also flattered me by using my name every so often. To most of us, our name is the most important sound in the English language and we warm to people who use it. I liked Don and wanted to get to know him better. Vanity, you might say. All he did was show an interest in me. Perhaps it was, but next time I talk with Don I am determined to draw him out so I may learn more about him. We have, I think, the beginning of a friendship.

FIND SOMETHING TO LIKE IN OTHER PEOPLE

Don made me feel good, primarily through showing interest in my activities and encouraging me to talk about myself. There are other ways of achieving this end, too. Probably the most obvious is to pay direct, personal compliments. However, such praise is more effective when made indirectly or subtly. It is good to feel that someone else admires us, particularly in a society where it seems to be more acceptable to put oneself down rather than to claim that one does something well. Such compliments should be genuine, but it is not really so hard to find something about a person worthy of praise. It is just a matter of looking. Try to avoid being put off by the prejudices of some third person, but look at everyone you meet in a positive way. Find something to like and admire rather than something to dislike. As William Arthur Ward put it: 'It is fair to judge people and stained-glass windows only in their best light.' This can be done on a large scale. Art Buchwald wrote a delightful little piece in the *Washington Post* entitled 'Love And The Cabbie', which illustrates this perfectly. Buchwald and a friend were travelling by cab in New York. When they reached their destination, as well as paying the fare, Buchwald told the driver how much he had enjoyed the trip and his expertise at the wheel. Typically, the driver, hardened by long exposure to New Yorkers, retored: 'Are you some kind of nut, or something?' Buchwald persisted, saying he had really appreciated his ride in the taxi. Though the driver went off shaking his head, he had a smile on his face. The columnist's friend inquired what was going on.

Buchwald explained his idea. If, during the day, he found something to compliment people about, he could make them feel better. Because they felt good they would be more inclined to say nice things to others with whom they came in contact. Like ripples in a pond, good feelings would expand. The friend, acting as so many of us do, raised objections, primarily that compliments would have no effect on lots of people. Buchwald admitted this was true, but claimed that if he found something to praise in ten people during the course of a day, at least two or three would respond positively. These two or three would interact with dozens of others during the day and, in turn, make two or three feel good, and so on. It is such a simple idea really. One that works well, too. You could do a lot worse than try it. There is a lot of personal satisfaction in knowing you have helped to make someone else's day better.

OTHER WAYS OF EGO BOOSTING

Another way of boosting the egos of those around you is to ask for advice, information, directions or opinions. This is really a form of flattery, for the implication is that the other person has access to knowledge which you do not possess. People crave appreciation and recognition, therefore by asking, either for information or for a favour, you please the other person by making him feel important. The request appeals to his vanity and will normally make him disposed to help you. It also encourages him to react favourably towards you as a person. So it is a good idea to let other people do you favours. When a person invests money or advice in you, he usually takes an interest in you. Let your behaviour reflect your belief that the advice is important to you.

Build up the people you associate with by imputing knowledge to them whether or not you know they possess it. Comments such as: 'I suppose you've done that lots of times already, but it's new to me' and 'I haven't visited the Middle East, but I imagine you know quite a lot about it' will make them feel good. Obviously, this approach can appear insincere. Often it is, of course, but your attempts to build relationships are likely to be crowned with more success if you are genuinely interested in the other person. An interest you contrive tends to be rather shallow. Usually, too, it is readily detected as such by the person to whom you are talking. Genuine interest is the essential, but the general principle still remains valid.

If you want to cement friendly relationships between yourself and others, the basic formula is to build up the other person's ego. Do not inflate your own ego at his expense through criticism. If you are honest with yourself you will see that the reason you do criticize others is to pull them down to — or lower than — your own level. When we think badly of ourselves, seeing ourselves as inadequate and unsuccessful, we often tend to look for weaknesses in others so we can make ourselves feel better at their expense. The price you pay is loss of friendship. So if you want to make and keep friends, avoid criticizing them.

Criticism, however, may be seen in a different way. Constructive criticism, designed to help other people, can be a sign of genuine friendship. Often, when we are behaving in a self-destructive way, we need someone to tell us so, firmly and forcefully. We may not like this advice, nor may we accept it, but without it the possibility of changing our behaviour is greatly reduced. The difficulty is distinguishing between this positive use of criticism and the more negative use which is probably more common. On your own part, whenever you are tempted to criticize, it might be just as well to ask yourself: 'Am I genuinely trying to be helpful, or am I trying to score points?' If you are honest with yourself, and your answer is that of point-scoring, hopefully you will refrain from voicing the criticism. In *The Laughing Cavalier* by Alan Turpin, we find this enlightening little exchange:

'You're very easy going', I said in some wonder.
'Well yes, I think that one learns one has to be. It seems to me that people's own actions usually teach them the lesson, so why should we add to their burden.'

Turpin has a point. Perhaps we could learn from it.

ACCEPT OTHERS AS THEY ARE

Yet, it is difficult to let other people be themselves. We feel that we must improve on them. Margaret Birney had been married for about three months when I overheard her, quite by chance, talking to my daughter. She mentioned certain things about her new husband to which she objected, but said quite confidently that she would soon change all that. She had been quite aware of these 'faults' before their marriage but said nothing, resolving to mould her husband once she was in a stronger position. How often we hear such comments. Why marry someone if you cannot accept him as he is? Love is the answer. Right. If you love somebody, you love him for what he is, so why try and change him into something else? Often, in fact, if you are successful in effecting the change you want, you find you are no longer in love with the person he becomes. Men are, of course, just as prone to acting in this way as are women. Neither sex has any monopoly on virtue in this context, both often trying to improve upon their mates, to make them over into an image that they find more acceptable. Lao-tsze, a Chinese philosopher, captured the spirit of the point I am trying to make:

If I keep from meddling with people,
they will take care of themselves.
If I keep from commanding people,
they will behave themselves.
If I keep from preaching at people,
they will improve themselves.
If I keep from improving on people,
they become themselves.

Accept other people as they are, accentuate the things you have in common, minimize those which divide you, and you have the basis for a lasting friendship.

MAKING AND KEEPING FRIENDS

Virtually everything I have been talking about in this chapter reflects my belief that friendship does not just happen. It requires a positive effort to make and keep friends. It helps if you *show you like them*. Smiles, compliments, acceptance, all contribute towards this impression. By making them feel good by your words and your actions, you demonstrate your liking for them. *Be warm*. Often you must initiate interactions without waiting for the other person. If you feel there is someone you would like to meet but have not yet done so, introduce yourself. Get their name right, be warm and cheerful. If you hang back expecting the other person or some third party to bring you together you might grow old waiting. Your boldness may be disastrous. That is the risk you take. Often it is not. The other person is just as eager as you for human interactions. Follow up the initial meeting with a note or phone call. Show your interest, your acceptance.

Perhaps you might be worried that you will have nothing to talk about. However, if you get the other person talking, and you pay attention to what he is saying, you should have no real problem here. Probe until you find the other person's interest. A useful way to achieve this was suggested by Crane in his book *Psychology Applied*, when he presented the DEAR HOME PALS approach to getting people talking. This formula provides a mnemonic cue to help a person remember a wide variety of topics suitable for conversation:

D =drama: movies, stage (e.g. favourite actors, actresses)
E =entertainment: recreation (e.g. chess, hiking)
A =athletics: various sports
R =relatives: family, early home environment

H =hobbies: present or childhood
O =occupation: home, children, job
M =music: type (e.g. do you play an instrument?)
E =engineering: cars, television, stereo, hi-fi

P =politics
A =appearance (e.g. compliments on dress)
L =literature
S =sex differences (e.g. do men and women have similar interests, talents, aptitudes?)

For those of us who might find the task of remembering three words too great, Crane provided a shorter conversational topics formula, appropriately entitled HELP.

H = hobbies
E = entertainment
L = literature
P = politics

With these key words memorized, you should have little trouble in keeping the conversational ball rolling.

Listening to what the other person tells you is, of course, absolutely vital. Try to be empathic, putting yourself in his shoes, seeing things from his point of view. Encourage him to speak, show your interest in what he has to say, and curb your own talkativeness to give him room to tell you something of himself. If you really want to find out what another person is like, this is most important.

Yet, there are appropriate times for us to carry our share of the talking. This raises a further point which, though not explicitly stated in previous chapters, has been implied on a number of occasions. *Show something of yourself to the other person*. This can be risky. When I let someone else see me as I really am, he may reject me. Perhaps I am so worthless that there is nothing about me to like. Therefore, I had better play it safe and confine myself to superficialities. If you do this, your chances of developing a meaningful relationship are slight. You will have acquaintances but not friends. For, as you disclose important things about yourself, deeply held beliefs, feelings about yourself as a person, your insecurities, your triumphs, you allow the other person to share these and to respond in the same way. You encourage him to give more of himself to the relationship and so the mutual growth continues. Being able to share the things that are really important to you with someone else is essential. It is the basis of enduring friendship.

Friendship, or more generally, the building of personal relationships, may be seen then as a deliberate matter. Phillips and Metzger, in their book *Intimate Communication*, certainly see it as such, guiding the whole process by precisely formulated goals. They claim it is rather useless to set up a goal such as: 'I want to be more effective in my relationship with Tom Smith.' This they see as too vague to be of any value as a guide to behaviour. To be successful the goal must be as precise as:

Over a period of time, not exceeding one year, I want to maintain a regular relationship with Tom. I will make sure to contact him at least twice a week, to generate at least one shared activity per week, and to respond to his invitations regularly. If I begin to hear from him at regular intervals, like once a week, during which time he also initiates shared activities, then I will be convinced that my relationship with him has improved.

On first reading the Phillips and Metzger approach, I reacted rather negatively. It seems so mechanical and manipulative. Yet, it does make a certain amount of sense. Usually we let slip opportunities for building relationships through our own laziness. Friendship grows through contact, and maintaining this constancy of contact requires effort. Perhaps through having a goal before us, such as the one set out above, we will be spurred into making the effort, into deliberately planning activities to advance the relationship. If this is so, the goal-setting approach may not be as 'unhumanistic' as it might appear on first meeting.

EFFICIENT PERSUASION

We are all salesmen. Perhaps you cannot agree with this statement, but I think it does express a basic truth. In one way or another all of us are selling something at some time. The girl working in a department store sells lingerie; the academic lecturing to his students sells ideas; and the man applying for a job is selling his ability. In our inter-personal relationships we sell ourselves as a human being capable of loving and worthy of being loved. Persuasion is a part of selling, a very big part, and it is valuable to consider how we might become more efficient in its use.

Although earlier in this chapter I suggested that acceptance of the other person is important for the establishment of close interpersonal relationships, there are times when it is necessary to attempt to win someone to your way of thinking. Often we try to do this through argument, attempting to convince the other person that our position is so compelling that he must surely see the need to change his viewpoint. The catch is that usually the other party to the argument is equally convinced of the correctness of his own position. An immovable object meets an irresistible force and nothing but ill-feeling is generated. I do not think anyone really wins arguments. The 'loser' often pays only lip-service to the 'superior' case advanced, secretly clinging even more strongly to his own viewpoint, and harbouring resentment against his adversary. This is because in an argument people are adversaries committed to maintaining certain positions. Giving these up is a loss of face, to be avoided at all cost. Rationality, then, has little chance of survival. If you doubt this, remember some of your own domestic arguments, or those with friends on politics and religion.

THE TECHNIQUES OF PERSUASION

Terry Sanderson is one of the most persuasive people I know. When I talk with him, everything seems so reasonable, so pleasant, that I find myself saying 'yes, yes' very quickly. That is part of his technique. He starts with points no one could possibly deny so he gains your agreement. This sets the scene, establishes the pattern the discussion will follow, for Terry is a very friendly fellow. He is courteous, too. He respects my opinion and would never come out blatantly saying I was wrong. Rather, he would let me do a lot of the talking, putting in a question here and there, until I would begin to see flaws in my own argument. This is the crux of persuasion. Instead of attempting to force people to see the superior logic of your own case, let them persuade themselves that you have a point worth considering.

Questions are a good way of doing this. Seeking clarification, for example: 'You mean that if I was to follow your advice here I should invest my money in the concrete industry?' Or almost thinking aloud about implications: 'That's interesting. If I take your point to its logical conclusion I would have to sell out of my real estate holdings?' Often quiet questions like these provoke a retraction from the other person. He has not really thought the thing through and, because you are not pressuring him, he is able to modify his position without loss of face.

This use of the question as a persuasive device had been of great help to me. Part of my university work involves advising academic staff on their teaching procedures with a view to helping them improve their performance. Many lecturers see me as a threat. They feel I am sitting in judgement, criticizing them as people. When I discuss their teaching with them, perhaps after viewing them present a lecture, I shall usually concentrate on asking them why they did certain things, rather than telling them about better ways of handling their material. Usually they will express dissatisfaction with some aspect of their performance, and ask me if I have any suggestions for improvement. I can then offer these without seeming to be forcing the issue.

Terry Sanderson does this too. He tries to put himself in the other person's shoes so that he can see things from their angle. This is an attempt to exchange minds with the person you are trying to influence, and it helps you to be sympathetic with his ideas. Sometimes, when you do this, you realize you are wrong in your own views. When Terry feels this way he admits it immediately. I admire that about him. It gives me confidence that if I do change my opinions as a result of my discussions with him I probably have been given good grounds for doing so.

I suppose Terry's basic technique is that he lets the other person talk himself out, and then suggests ways in which the difficulties which have arisen could be resolved. This turns into a co-operative enterprise where a viewpoint, once held with unshakable convication, is modified in accordance with another person's insights. When persuasion is used in this non-coercive way, it is a valuable learning experience for both parties. It also cements friendly relations instead of engendering the bitterness of normal argumentation.

7. Solving Problems & Making Decisions

In previous chapters I have talked about problems which arise in the course of our everyday life. Solving these problems is a matter of making decisions, and this chapter will outline some of the ways in which you can go about this task. Both conscious and subconscious mental processes will be considered, for each of these can be utilized in rather different ways. For most people, however, problem-solving would be seen as a very rational procedure, drawing on the reasoning powers of the conscious mind. Accordingly, we shall begin with a consideration of this approach.

PROBLEM-SOLVING AND DECISION-MAKING AS A RATIONAL PROCESS

Joanna and Peter Norman were trying to decide on the purchase of a block of land. Since their marriage three years earlier, they had been living with Joanna's family and they now felt the need to create their own home. Buying a block of land was the first step in meeting the need. However, deciding on which particular block was somewhat of a problem. Factors such as price, size and location were all important, so the Normans spent many hours weighing up the alternative merits of the blocks which were on offer. Weekends were occupied with inspections, discussions with agents, and imagining the type of home which could be constructed on particular sites. Finally, Joanna and Peter made their decision. They purchased a block which seemed to meet their needs reasonably well. Not that it was perfect. Perfection is a rare commodity. However, it did provide a sensible compromise between what they wanted, what they could afford, and what was available.

Several months later, Peter was talking with a casual business acquaintance. The subject of land came up. Peter's acquaintance happened to mention his sister's troubles with her new home. Because of the presence of underground springs, the land on which her house was built seemed to be subsiding. Despite solid foundations, cracks were appearing in the walls, causing her a lot of distress. Coincidentally, the location of this house was very close to that of the block Peter now owned. Further investigation confirmed the existence of these springs and it seemed very likely that any home built on the Normans' land would also run the risk of subsidence. In the light of this new evidence Joanna and Peter changed their decision. Fortunately they were able to sell their block. Their second choice proved a more fortunate one and all went well with their home when it was built.

There are several steps involved in the process of solving a problem and coming to a decision. The Normans' experience outlined above illustrates these. Initially, there was a felt need, the desire to strike out on their own. Most problems begin with such a felt need, perhaps reflected as a state of doubt or frustration. Maybe it involves an awareness of a difficulty which should be resolved. From this felt need comes an attempt to identify the problem, to get clear the end point which is desired. In the case of Joanna and Peter, this goal was the creation of their new home. As a sub-goal, location and purchase of a suitable building block was the specific end point.

Sometimes actually identifying the problem is the key to its solution. It is quite likely that the Normans experienced vague, ill-defined feelings of disquiet, uneasiness and tension for some time before they actually pin-pointed what was the cause of their disturbance. Once they realized that living in the same house as Joanna's parents was the problem, they could take definite steps to seek a solution. Talking over your situation with another person may often help you clarify your thoughts when you are uncertain about what it is that is actually troubling you. Going for a walk and talking out loud to yourself, though it may startle any passers-by, is another way of achieving this clarification. Alternatively, you could use free association to reveal your problem. Sit down comfortably with a pencil and paper, jotting down words, one suggesting the next. Or you may prefer to talk into a tape recorder. Obviously, nothing can be achieved, no decision arrived at, until you are quite clear about what your problem is. The more clearly you can state the nature of your difficulty, the more likely you are to solve it. Once you have achieved this, the next step is to collect as much pertinent information as possible. This enables you to consider facts, rather than relying solely upon prejudice or tradition.

You will never be able to collect *all* the information bearing on your particular problems. In fact, if you continually postpone making a decision on the grounds that there may be still more information available which you have not yet secured, you run the risk of being like the gentleman in the Chinese proverb: 'He who deliberates fully before taking a step will spend his entire life on one leg.' So, accumulate as much data as you can without worrying too much whether you have it all. Draw on your background experience, the material gained from your reading, the information derived from other people, to formulate a number of possible solutions. From these you attempt to select the alternative most likely to be successful. Perhaps a series of questions would help you make this decision. Will this achieve my goal? Is it realistic? How much will it cost? Will I hurt anyone if I solve my problem this way? Who might object to it? Writing down the arguments for and against a particular solution is likely to help too. This makes it more concrete, easier to work with.

This 'best solution' can be considered as a tentative guess about the probable result of a particular situation, based on a certain amount of factual information. Joanna and Peter considered a number of blocks of land, comparing them in terms of cost, location, size and general appeal, until they were able to make a choice. This was their best guess in the light of the information they had available. They then went ahead and purchased the land. Their decision was made, their problem solved.

Normally, the next step, in the rational approach to problem-solving, is to test the 'best solution'. This may involve predicting the consequences of the tentative proposal or perhaps giving it a trial run. The Normans made some attempt to do the first of these, trying out their solution on other people, asking for opinions about their choice. These were positive, so they were confirmed in the decision. Having a test-run was not really possible. They could not build a house and then refuse to buy the land because of the difficulties which might eventuate. However, they were lucky. In fact, they did 'test' their purchase, found it wanting in the light of information they did not originally possess, and were fortunate enough to escape unscathed from their poor choice. They were then free to arrive at another 'best solution'.

In summary, then, a useful approach to decision-making can be organized around a series of questions:

What is the problem?
Define it and set it down on paper.
Is the problem too big to tackle?
If so, divide it into sub-problems and tackle one aspect at a time.
What information do I have?
Draw on relevant background ideas and previously achieved problem solutions. Use your past experience, organizing and reorganizing it to bear on the present problem.
What additional information do I need?
Collect this by personal inquiry, reading, discussion.

What are the possible solutions to the problem?
What is the best solution?
Take positive action and put this into effect.
Did the solution work?
If not, decide on another solution to try out.

The use of a strategy such as that set out above brings with it a sense of purpose, an expectation that the problem can be solved rationally. This feeling of confidence is likely to produce positive results. Having a plan of attack is eminently preferable to floundering helplessly, a prey to frustration and despair. It is not really the problems we have which upset us. Rather it is our lack of faith in our ability to solve them.

DRAMATIZE YOUR DECISION-MAKING SITUATIONS

Often this lack of faith is a result of coping with problems in an abstract way, keeping everything in our heads where it goes round and round and round, churning up our insides with worry. Above (p. 96), I mentioned the simple device of writing things down: when faced with a decision, list the various arguments for and against your possible choices. This helps you clarify the issues. So, too, does dramatizing the choice situation.

John Holmes has a problem. Actually, it is one many men would like to have. Two girls are in love with him. Both want to marry him. John wants to get married, too, but he finds it virtually impossible to make a choice. When he is with Beth, he is convinced she is the girl for him. Her wit, beauty and sensitivity delight him. Yet, when he is with Pauline, her joyous sense of fun and sheer delight in living help him feel vibrantly alive. The more John compares the two girls in his mind, when apart from them, the more confused he becomes. He feels the time is ripe to settle down, make a home, raise a family, yet he is unable to make a decision.

One possible solution to John's problem lies in the creation of a dramatic situation involving Beth and Pauline. Not a real life situation, but one he can build in his own mind. There is an accident. Both girls are badly hurt, hovering near death. Chances of survival are slim. How does John feel about this? Can he envisage his life without both Beth and Pauline with equanimity? Or could he bear the loss of one of them more easily than the other? As pointed out above, the imagination is very powerful and it is possible to engender a frightening realism in a situation such as that outlined. Often, the decision makes itself clear under these conditions. The 'best solution' becomes obvious. For John, the thought of life without Pauline was unbearable. He married her.

BRAINSTORMING FOR
CREATIVE SOLUTIONS

Dramatizing a situation to aid decision-making could be seen as a rather creative approach, something which is often lacking in rational problem-solving, where the emphasis usually falls upon convergent thinking. This is a type of thinking directed towards producing the one correct answer and is relatively conventional in nature. In their book, *Creativity and Intelligence*, Getzels and Jackson quote this story produced by a student categorized as a convergent thinker. The stimulus for the story was a picture of a man reclining in an airplane on his return from a business trip or professional conference:

Mr. Smith is on his way home from a successful business trip. He is very happy and is thinking about his wonderful family and how glad he will be to see them again. He can picture it, about an hour from now, his plane landing at the airport and Mrs. Smith and their children all there welcoming him home again.

A neat conventional tale of a family reunion, quite different in nature from the following story produced by a divergent thinker:

This man is flying back from Reno, where he has just won a divorce from his wife. He couldn't stand to live with her any more, he told the judge, because she wore so much cold cream on her face at night that her head would skid across the pillow and hit him in the head. He is now contemplating a new skidproof face cream.

Both stories were based on the same picture, yet the second one reveals a greater range of response. It seems more creative. 'Creativity' is a difficult word to define but, in the present context of problem-solving and decision-making, I shall use it to mean originality, the ability to produce unusual ideas and solutions. This is not easy to do. When faced with a problem we tend to come up with fairly conventional, unoriginal ways of handling it. We need some means of breaking out of this pattern, some method which virtually pushes us beyond the conventional answer into more fanciful and less inhibited realms.

Brainstorming is such a method. Its great strength is the way in which the generation of ideas is separated from their evaluation. Usually, when we produce an idea we immediately consider its value. Is it an answer to the particular problem? Is it good? Is it bad? As a result, many potentially valuable ideas die still-born, killed by the icy blast of instant judgement. This is true whether the judgement is passed by yourself, when wrestling individually with your problems, or whether it is passed by members of a group who are involved in co-operative decision-making. This does not occur when brainstorming is used.

If a number of people are concerned to find the answer to a particular problem, they simply contribute as many ideas as possible. As a solution is suggested it is written on a board, or on a sheet of paper, which is pinned up so all can see. Criticism is absolutely barred at this time, no matter how odd the contribution may seem. Combination of ideas is encouraged, with one person building on the suggestions of others. It is quantity that is sought, the theory being that once the conventional solutions are exhausted, people will start coming up with unusual, remote, wild solutions which normally would never see the light of day.

Once the stream of suggestions dries up, evaluation begins. Everything written on the board or paper is considered in relation to the problem which must be solved. Further combining and re-combining takes place until agreement is reached on the best solution. Often, as a result of this separation of idea generation and idea evaluation, the solution is more creative than the conventional ones first suggested. This is not to claim that such an idea will necessarily be more successful. It may not be. However, without the brainstorming approach to force thinking into more original channels, the conventional, convergent solution usually prevails, and this may not always be desirable.

Even without a group of people, brainstorming may still be used. Dale Harvey, an author of my acquaintance, employs it to solve problems he may be having with his plots. Perhaps he has become stuck at a particular point in his story. He cannot see the direction in which he should go. So Dale sits down, turns on his tape recorder, and talks. First he talks about the story as far as it has progressed, then he poses the problem. Where do I go from here? He tries to think of many possibilities, without any real regard for their practicability. When the flow of ideas ceases, Dale gets up, wanders around the room, looks out of the window, perhaps does an isometric exercise or two, and returns to his chair. Usually more suggestions emerge. If they do not he commences pacing for, like so many of us, he thinks effectively while he is moving. Ultimately, he feels he has exhausted the range of possibilities. He leaves his tape until next day, at which time he begins evaluating the mass of ideas he has generated. Some he can eliminate immediately, others require a little more consideration, and others again emerge as distinct possibilities. These he uses as starting-points for a fresh brainstorming session, which usually gives him the problem solution.

THE PROCESS OF CREATIVE THINKING

Creative thinking can be encouraged in ways other than brainstorming. The person who would like to arrive at more unusual, and possibly more effective, solutions to his problems could do a lot worse than to make use of the following plan which embraces preparation, incubation, illumination and verification.

Preparation means the absorption of information pertinent to the problem. The points made above about problem identification, collection of facts, and generation of possible solutions are relevant here. It is a matter of collecting together as much data as possible, studying it, asking yourself questions, immersing yourself in it.

Then comes incubation, a turning-off process whereby the material is put aside. There is a release from the pressure of fact gathering and studying, this being replaced by a period of quiet, of waiting for the ideas to mature. The ideas are not abandoned, but are turned over in the mind every so often in a very leisurely, unhurried way. No attempt is made to force the solution. In this quiet time of relaxation, ideas can be assimilated in the thought processes, information can be rearranged, and various possible solutions either rise to prominence or recede into insignificance.

Illumination comes next. This is often a flash of insight, an 'ah ha' experience whereby the solution emerges full blown in the mind. There is a clear conception of the best answer to the problem, the best decision to take.

Finally, as with our earlier problem-solving plan, verification is necessary. The brilliant idea must be put into practice to find out whether it actually works. Perhaps, before this is done, there may be further rethinking to improve the 'best solution', a reworking to smooth out some rough edges.

To some extent this is the process Dale Harvey used. His brainstorming activity produced the necessary data, and this was followed by a day of quiet away from this material. As he reworked the data he had generated, the 'best solution' emerged. This was then verified when he resumed work on his story. Actually, his incubation period provided an opportunity for his subconscious mind to help him arrive at a decision. Making use of such subconscious mental processes can usually improve the quality of our decisions, and it is to a consideration of their contribution to problem-solving that we now turn.

USING THE SUBCONSCIOUS MIND IN PROBLEM-SOLVING

John Chilton Pearce has pointed out that the rational problem-solving processes of the conscious mind do not provide a complete answer:

Problem-solving is like patching holes in a rotten boat; for each patch applied two more leaks spring up. There are times when we need a way beyond rotten hulks, a way not for restructuring a new boat or even a serviceable life jacket, but rather some sub-mariner's way through a sea of confusion to new terrain.

Pearce's 'way out' might be through the use of the subconscious mind to provide solutions that are somewhat out of the ordinary. It has often been suggested that if you are struggling with a problem, and no answers are coming, you could do well to relax, to simply turn off the conscious mind and let the subconscious take over. As you do so, you adopt an attitude of optimism. That is, you expect answers to come in the course of your daily activities. Perhaps they will arrive through a chance remark, an intuitive flash while enjoying your morning shower, or through a thought picked up at random from a song, a book, a magazine or newspaper.

With an expectation of success, you tend to see opportunities, clues, solutions which previously passed you by. These must be noted down immediately they occur, for the fleeting idea can depart as quickly as it arrived. Carrying a notebook is a useful habit to cultivate in this regard. Once the 'flash' has been recorded you may like to let it mature a little before acting upon it. Frequently, one such intuitive idea triggers another until you have many possible problem solutions available for consideration.

Ron Harrison used this method. He had a problem. Recently elected as president of his local Rotary Club branch, he was required to deliver a speech at the next meeting. Unused to public speaking, Ron was apprehensive about his task. For days he fretted. What should he talk about? Finally, he decided to turn the problem of content over to his subconscious mind.

Ron had an intense interest in his problem and had defined it clearly, both important prerequisites for the particular approach he was going to use. He talked to various members of his club, particularly past presidents and those with some public-speaking experience, securing as much information as possible. In a relaxed state, he visualized the end result. He 'saw' himself speaking to the group and 'heard' them congratulating him on an excellent performance. He then told his subconscious mind he wanted ideas outlining what he should talk about in order to achieve that end result. This is akin to issuing instructions on what is required, specifying that the solution-finding process is to go on underground without conscious awareness. Ron trusted his subconscious mind to come up with the answer by a particular date which he set. Really the only thing that could have prevented his success was attempting to force the process through too much conscious effort. Often anxiety can cause this, but Ron was able to let the subconscious mind work for him in its own way.

He got his answer. Two days later, as he was waiting to see his doctor, he idly flipped over several magazines in the waiting room. A particular article caught his eye and fired his enthusiasm as he read it. Several books were mentioned in the article and Ron read these too. When he gave his speech he was full of enthusiasm and zest, probably the most valuable attributes of any speaker. So involved was he in this subject he forgot all about himself. His success was assured. Coincidence? Perhaps, but after one sees such coincidences occurring again and again, once the subconscious mind is instructed to solve problems, one seriously doubts this explanation. The very act of invoking subconscious processes seems to sensitize us so that appropriate things start happening; we recognize answers and opportunities where apparently none existed before.

Ron gave instructions to his subconscious mind. Bertrand Russell is reported to have adopted the same approach. When he wished to write a book he would collect all the material he had available, think about it, and then hand it over to his subconscious mind, instructing it to be ready to write the book by a certain date. He then would put away his file or material and devote his attention to other matters. From time to time, ideas about his proposed book would occur to him and these he would include in his ever-growing file. When the designated date arrived Russell would bring out his file, review the material it contained, and proceed to write his book.

Alternatively, instead of instructing your subconscious you might prefer to question it. As you allow yourself to relax, you open your mind to guidance. You ask yourself questions designed to provide a sense of direction. After reviewing the ideas you have about a particular problem or situation, you might ask: 'What is my next step? Where do I go from here?' and passively await an answer. Perhaps you might wish to invoke the concept of a 'guide' or 'counsellor'. Try to think of somebody who is likely to have the answer to your problem. It may be an historical figure, a minister, a doctor, a teacher, a guru, anyone at all. As you relax, visualize this person, attempting to 'see' him or her as vividly as possible. Again, you ask your question and wait patiently for an answer.

You may prefer not to pre-select a guide. In this case relax and, in your mind, go to a place where you feel comfortable. It might be your tranquillity room, a lake, a forest, a beach, anywhere where you feel at peace. As you create this world in your mind, wait for a person to appear. When he or she does, explain why you have come and why you need help. Let yourself be at ease with your creation, seeing it as an adviser, a friend. When you feel comfortable, ask your question. If no answer is forthcoming, probe further, requesting your guide to tell you how you might solve your problem.

Fanciful? Probably. Yet it can be a very helpful means of making decisions. If it works for you, do not worry too much about what your friends or family might say. They may choose to ridicule you for believing such nonsense, but if you improve your decision-making ability, the gain is yours. By cutting themselves off from the possibility of more creative problem solutions, they are the losers. On the other hand, if you get nowhere with the approach, forget it. The main thing to bear in mind with all the suggestions put forward in this book is that they are things for you to try out. Those that help you, use them; those that do not, let them go. Just try to keep an open mind so that you will give them a trial before you reject them. By deciding beforehand that something will not work, we deprive ourselves of many things which might enhance our lives.

THE TIME WHEN WE FALL
ASLEEP CAN BE USEFUL TOO

To many people, the hours when we are asleep are a prodigious waste of valuable time. Nothing happens. Nothing is accomplished. Yet these hours may be used very productively. The subconscious mind never sleeps. It continues to work on the material gathered during the day and the material stored over our entire lifetime. You can deliberately programme your subconscious mind to work for you while you sleep. Before going to bed, select an 'incubating' idea and think intensely about it, exploring its implications. Perhaps it is a problem to which you are seeking a solution, a decision you must make. Having done your period of hard thinking, put it aside and retire for the night. Be sure you have a pen and paper beside the bed.

During the night, it is quite likely you will awake with your solution completely worked out, for your subconscious mind has been busy with the problem as you slept. This solution may not remain in your mind till morning, so it is necessary to write it down immediately. On the other hand, it is equally likely that you will spend an undisturbed restful night, awakening at your usual time in the morning. Perhaps your answer will come to you at this point. Maybe not. I frequently receive my answers while I am shaving but the process cannot be hurried. The solutions will come if you wait patiently. If you wish, you can do as Bertrand Russell did: talk to your subconscious mind as if it were a separate entity, telling it to provide the answer while you sleep.

You will notice a similarity between this approach and that described under the heading of creative thinking. Problem-solving is a blend of conscious and subconscious processes. It is not, then, a question of using one way or the other, but more of striking a balance to help you arrive at the best solution as efficiently as possible. The key concepts are, first, to consciously formulate your problems and fill your mind with every bit of information about it that you can, and second, to relax, letting your mind dwell on it for a few moments before you turn it over to the subconscious with a 'you work out the answer' instruction. Nowhere has the applicability of this procedure been more clearly demonstrated than in the area of business decision-making.

TOO MANY HOURS, TOO LITTLE PRODUCED

In several articles written more than fifty years ago, Robert Updegraff expressed the idea that most business executives work too many hours of the day and, as a result of this, accomplish too little. On first glance this statement seems somewhat self-contradictory, yet its meaning becomes clear as Updegraff explains why he feels this is so. It is because little time is allowed for use of the subconscious mind. As Updegraff puts it:

When a man takes a position with a business in an executive or administrative capacity, he brings with him a two-part mind; conscious and subconscious. The business that employs him is entitled to the services of both parts of his mind, but in far too many cases it gets the benefit of only one. The conscious mind goes on the payroll as a matter of course, but the subconscious mind, which as a rule does far the better work, is allowed to loaf. (*Taking Subconscious Mind Into Business*).

The reason why the subconscious mind is likely to contribute so little is because it is given no chance to do otherwise. The reason for this may be found in a wrong concept of work which is seen as hours spent at a desk, as conscientious application; as activity; as business. Yet, as Updegraff points out, the only purpose of an office is to serve the function of a contact point, or centre of operations for putting into effect the decisions, plans, and ideas arrived at in one's mind, consciously or subconsciously. If this concept can be accepted, it seems unnecessary for a certain specified number of hours each day to be spent at a desk. A desk is not a thinking machine. Quite the contrary, in fact. Cluttered as they usually are with papers, they are likely to provide a distraction, an impediment to constructive thought. They are the place where an executive gets so close to his business that he is unable to gain a clear perspective on it. Desk-bound thinking, Updegraff claims, is probably responsible for more poor decisions than lack of business ability.

He would go further, extending his criticism of desk-bound thinking to conscious decision-making in general. Based on a twenty-year observation of business men, Updegraff asserts that most of their wrong moves—caused by wrong decisions—have occurred when they have tried hardest to be rational and logical. Yet those decisions which seemed to have arisen almost intuitively are frequently correct, despite the fact that they may initially have appeared to be quite illogical. A possible explanation of these observed facts is that conscious problem-solving based on reasoning often leaves out some vital factor; whereas intuitive decisions arising from subconscious mental processes seem to embrace the whole underlying process of life.

DECISION-MAKING IN BUSINESS

How, then, can the subconscious mind be taken into business? Updegraff's solution is quite revolutionary. Work a six-hour day. This six-hour period is to include the luncheon period and is to be devoted to conscious and concentrated application to the problems and human contacts of the job. At three o'clock, the executive is to retire for the day, allowing the subconscious mind to take over the load. How is it to do so? By trying not to work. If he cannot actually leave the office at three o'clock, the executive at least avoids doing anything likely to impose any strain on his subconscious mind. As we have seen, relaxation is the key to the subconscious mind, which performs most effectively when the consciously imposed pressure is off. The wonderful thing about it is that it works best when we are doing the things we enjoy—dancing, reading novels, playing sport, listening to music.

Updegraff, then, is expressing the idea of balancing the day's work between the conscious and subconscious minds, so that the latter carries a larger share than it is normally permitted to do. There is a time for intense concentration and application; there is also a time to relax. In his *Journal*, Henry David Thoreau expressed this same idea when he wrote:

The really efficient labourer will be found not to crowd his day with work, but will saunter to his tasks surrounded by a wide halo of ease and leisure. There will be a wide margin for relaxation in his day. He is only earnest to secure the kernels of time, and does not exaggerate the value of the husk. Why should the hen sit all day long? She can lay but one egg, and beside she will not have picked up materials for a good one. Those who work much do not work hard.

Thoreau's statement may easily be interpreted as an invitation to idleness. So, too, might Updegraff's six-hour-day idea. Yet, it is wise not to confuse activity with accomplishment. We do not necessarily achieve great things by rushing around energetically; nor do we necessarily waste our time by relaxing and doing the things we enjoy doing.

Still, consciously controlled thinking is vital as a stimulus to subconscious decision-making. Thinking can be, in fact, compared to a cooking process. This is another of Updegraff's ideas. He sees the mind as a cooker. Our conscious minds are the burners which start the process. Our subconscious mind is the oven in which the cooking is completed, working on stored heat. If we insist on doing all our 'mental' cooking consciously, we burn energy at a high rate. However, if we choose to use our subconscious mind to do the 'cooking' with retained heat, we are likely to be more efficient with far less wear and tear on the mind. This is because we are drawing upon past experience and stored knowledge while the problem 'cooks'.

When we present a definite problem to the subconscious mind we begin the 'cooking' process. However, we have prepared the ingredients by gathering all the necessary facts, organizing the data rationally, and thinking about possible solutions. Having 'pre-heated' the problem we then turn it over to the subconscious mind to simmer until cooked.

Lord Leverhulme has been often quoted as a man who employed this approach in the way he handled his correspondence. With a pile of letters before him, he would systematically work through them dictating as fast as possible. Occasionally he came to a letter he was unable to handle in this way. He could not think of an appropriate answer. Instead of wrestling with the problem at this time, he consciously organized the relevant facts and factors in his mind, and shifted the difficult letter to the bottom of the pile. He started the cooking process, then continued handling his mail. When the difficult letter came up again, he usually found he was able immediately to dictate a reply. His subconscious mind had provided the answers while his conscious mind was engaged with the other letters.

This process can be systemized very easily. Updegraff reduces it to a simple form as set out below:

Sub-conscious 'Cooker' Sheet

Date: October 10th   **Bring up:** Every Monday a.m.

Statement of the problem:

Tony Graham is not succeeding as a departmental head. Either we help him perform better or we dismiss him.

FIVE possible approaches to a solution:

1. Tell him he has only six months in which to demonstrate his ability to run his department.
2. Set up group meetings with other departmental heads to discuss common problems.
3. Meet with him informally to find out what his problems are and offer advice casually.
4. Praise him as often as possible.
5. Ask contacts in other companies what they do under similar circumstances.

These are my thoughts up to now:

— When we appointed him he seemed well qualified. What has happened to him — or has the job changed?

— He seems to lack interest. When we appointed him he was enthusiastic. Has he found the job dull?

— Lately Tony has been irritable, tired. Is he well physically? Perhaps he is having domestic problems?

— What part of the job is he doing well? What parts badly? How can I help him improve the bad parts?

— If I was in his shoes, how would I handle the job?

Precision is essential for 'statement of the problem'. Also brevity. No more than a sentence or two here to make it crystal clear. This 'turns on the heat'. Five possible approaches or solutions come next, followed by a section for jotting down ideas at random. This is a type of individual brainstorming when any idea is legitimate. By using the sheet in this way, conscious material is used to start the cooking process. No attempt is made to consciously answer the questions posed. That is the task of the subconscious mind. However, the subconscious mind can be reminded about its work every so often. That is the function of the 'bring up every Monday a.m.' entry in the top right-hand corner of the sheet. If no solution has spontaneously emerged by Monday morning, the sheet is re-read and any fresh ideas added. Once this 'stirring' has been completed, the problem is again handed over to the subconscious.

This cooking process works best when a clear specification is provided by the conscious mind. All the known data should be assembled and closely examined. Arguments for and against a particular decision should be set out and worked over in considerable detail. The desired end result, a problem solution, a decision, should be made very clear. Once the subconscious mind has such a clear target, it will usually provide the means of getting there.

APPLICATIONS OF THE 'COOKING' PROCESS

Joe Hargreaves, manager of an industrial tools factory, rather liked the idea of a six-hour day. Yet, he did not feel easy about leaving his office at three o'clock. Although, occasionally, he did head off for a game of golf, he was unable to completely rid himself of a certain guilt feeling. He felt obliged to be in his office from 9.00 a.m. to 5.00 p.m. every day, unless exceptional circumstances made this impossible. Such an obligation is, of course, part of the problem Undegraff (see p. 107) posed. In his eyes, Joe had a wrong concept of work which was interfering with his productivity.

Despite his strong sense of obligation, however, Joe did succeed in working a six-hour day. Through a rearrangement of his office furniture he was able to create two distinct areas. The first of these was his desk area. Here he exercised his conscious mind for six hours. At two o'clock he would work on his subconscious 'cooker sheets', setting out the problems to be solved, the questions needing answers, the decisions to be made. These were not necessarily of immediate importance. In fact, Joe would frequently 'fire his cooker' well in advance of the time when a decision was necessary. The problems he could see looming in the months ahead found their way onto his cooker sheets. By acting in this way, Joe found he could increase his effectiveness greatly, for when the difficult decision arrived, he was well prepared to make it.

At three o'clock Joe finished his six-hour day. He left his desk. Then he moved to the second area of his office. Here was a comfortable chair, a table, and a small bookcase. Joe loved westerns and crime stories yet, in the past, he had found little time for such frivolous reading. Now he put his feet up, turned off the office concerns, and lost himself in his books. Normally he was completely undisturbed, for he had made it clear to his staff and secretary that only matters of the direst urgency could come to him after three o'clock.

Very quickly Joe discovered that he needed a pad and pencil on his table. As he read of cowboy heroes and tough private detectives, thoughts concerning the subconscious cooker sheets arose spontaneously. These he jotted down without making any attempt to pursue them. He simply returned to his novels. Often complete solutions drifted into his mind. At other times, ideas about collecting additional information figured prominently. All were recorded to be considered next day during 'working hours'.

My own experience parallels closely that of Joe Hargreaves. I have created such a relaxation corner in my own office, though the books I read are more work-oriented. Still, they are usually quite different from the material upon which I am consciously working. When I become blocked in some task, I leave my desk, go to my easy chair, and start reading. Ideas about my task may or may not arise but, after a short time, I can return to my desk with a new slant on my material. The block has disappeared during my relocation period.

Taking this even further, when planning an article or a series of lectures, I may find my thoughts simply going around in circles. What I write down is poor, laboured and awkwardly worded. Continuing to work in this fashion is clearly unproductive. Yet, this is what so many of us do. We keep forcing the conscious mind even when it makes it quite clear to us that it has had enough. My answer, if it is a warm day, is to go out and lie in the sun. As I feel the warmth soaking into my body I relax completely. My mind drifts. Often within minutes the organizational structure I was unable to find arrives full blown. All that is necessary is to write it down, and I always keep a pad handy for this purpose. It is so easy and so pleasant. Yet, this sunbathing behaviour would be seen by many as loafing. It is in one sense, of course. In another sense, though, it is very work-effective behaviour because it quickly produces answers to questions which were frustrating me, and upon which I was wasting a lot of time.

Similarly, I use my pre-breakfast jog in the same way. Before I go I prime my subconscious mind with information about a decision I have to make, a question I have to answer. This very brief review completed, I then put it out of my mind and start jogging. Often, on my return I fill pages with ideas bearing on the problem which have come to me quite spontaneously as I ran. Again, a very time-efficient activity — exercise and decision-making combined.

Such examples may be multiplied many times over. Use those often wasted hours of travelling to and from work more productively. Start the cooking process by consciously feeding in the appropriate information, then turn off while you enjoy your walk to the station. During the train journey, while your conscious mind is occupied with the newspaper, your subconscious mind works on this information. By the time you arrive at work, you may have your answer. If not, you have lost nothing. It is a no-lose, possible-win situation, a comfortable position to be in, with decisions and problem solutions coming easily.

DECISION-MAKING AND STRESS

There is a very real need for easier, quicker decision-making. For many of my patients indecisiveness is the main reason for their anxiety and tension. Their greatest stress is experienced when the necessity for making a decision is forced upon them, and this happens many times every day. Literally, hundreds of times each day we have to make choices. If we do not do so quickly, we can spend hours agonizing over our decisions, with jumbled ideas chasing each other round and round our minds like rats on a treadmill. Even when we do resolve our problem, we then agonize over whether our decision was the correct one. No wonder we feel stressed and upset under such conditions.

Eve Bartols is very indecisive. She hates her shopping days. She loathes the supermarket. Why? Because of the number of decisions she has to make. Which products to buy? Which brands? How great a quantity? How much should she spend on a particular item? So many decisions, so much strain as a result. When she returns home, exhausted, Eve faces more decisions. What should she prepare for dinner? Should she take in the clothes from the line? They are not yet dry, but it might rain. And so on. Hundreds of decisions, day after day, week after week, year after year. Perhaps, herein lies one reason for the growing incidence of nervous breakdowns, and for the widespread belief that the era in which we now live is one of extreme stress.

Yet, most of the decisions Eve has to make are trivial. This is true of us all. Our decision really does not matter very much. So Eve does decide not to bring in the clothes and it rains. Is this so catastrophic? All that is necessary is to wait for some dry weather, or use a dryer, or dry them in front of a heater. Inconvenient maybe, disastrous no. But we carry on as if our wrong decisions are a calamity. What if Eve did choose badly at the supermarket? The world will not come to an end as a result of her poor decisions. It really is not all that important.

Furthermore, even if a decision is an important one, and a poor choice has been made, the situation is rarely beyond repair. Consider the illustration used to commence this chapter. Joanna and Peter Norman made a mistake. They made a wrong decision about buying a block of land. This decision was, however, reversible. They were able to avoid the consequences of their poor choice. Usually, we are able to do the same with our own choices, yet we rarely realize this. We feel we are committing ourselves for all time when we make our decisions, but this is simply not so. Most blunders are retrievable. Not all, but most. If you can accept that this is so, much of the strain will go out of decision-making. The sky will not fall in if you are wrong.

Still, a problem does exist. People do find it hard to make up their minds. They postpone decisions where possible, and continually equivocate, vacillating one way or the other depending on the mood of the moment. Is there some way of cutting through this indecision, of making decisions quickly and painlessly? I believe there is, and it involves the use of a pendulum.

THE PENDULUM

Your acceptance of the method to be now outlined will depend to some extent on your reaction to my earlier points about the triviality and reversibility of most of our decisions. If you are able to agree with this view, you may simply consider the use of a pendulum for decision-making as a convenient means of forcing a choice. On the other hand, if you prefer to think of the decisions you are called upon to make as being very important, you will probably reject the pendulum method as inappropriate. As I have stressed so often in this book, the choice is yours.

The pendulum may be any small object such as a ring, a key, a small piece of gemstone, a crystal, or a medallion. A thread, perhaps of nylon or cotton, is tied to this object. Length is usually about 20–25 centimetres. The thread is held between thumb and forefinger, about 5–8 centimetres from the pendulum bob. The remainder of the thread is wrapped around your fingers out of the way. With the pendulum thus suspended from your fingers, bend your elbow so that the forearm is approximately parallel with the ground. You may rest your elbow on a chair arm or table, but many people prefer to have the arm unsupported. I favour this myself.

Next, swing the pendulum about, to and fro, clockwise and anti-clockwise, keeping all movement of fingers, hand and arm to a minimum. As you do so, vary the length of the thread until you find a position which seems natural for you. This point is usually identifiable both through the feeling of 'rightness' and through the quick swing of the pendulum. Originally, I held my thread about 6 centimetres from the bob but lately find I get best results with a much shorter length, approximately 2 centimetres. Thus, the length with which you feel comfortable may vary from time to time. The important thing is that it feels 'right' for you, and that the pendulum bob moves about smoothly without you using any visible effort.

Four basic movements of the pendulum are possible. These are a back and forth movement in front of you, from left to right and right to left, across your body; a to-and-fro movement, towards your body and then away; a circular clockwise movement, and a circular anti-clockwise movement. Your inner mind can be asked to make its own selection from among those movements, so that a specific response is attached to each one. One movement is to signify 'yes', a second 'no', a third 'I don't know', and a fourth 'I don't want to answer the question'.

To sort out for yourself which movement means 'yes', ask the pendulum. Adopting an attitude of neutrality, of detachment, think 'yes' to yourself while watching the pendulum. Alternatively, you might, if your name is Stewart Riddle, ask: 'Is my name Stewart Riddle?' Observe the movement of the pendulum in response to this question. This is your 'yes' answer. Run a couple of tests to definitely establish this response. Then think 'no , or think of a name not your own, and ask 'Is my name Anthony Kilpatrick?' Again, repeat with another question or two to establish your 'no' movement. Now, try thinking 'I don't know' as you watch the pendulum. This establishes the third movement and obviously 'I don't want to answer this question' is the one remaining.

Another interesting way of identifying the 'yes' and 'no' responses is to hold the pendulum over a power cord connected to a piece of electrical equipment, a heater perhaps, or a toaster. Turn on the power and ask the pendulum whether a current is flowing through the cord. Then switch off the power and ask the same question. Whichever way you choose to establish your answers, the resultant movements will be constant for you. 'Yes' for me is always back and forth across my body; 'no' is always a to-and-fro motion.

Why does this occur? The theory is that you are establishing a code of communication through subconsciously controlled signals. The pendulum, in other words, is simply a device for gaining information from the subconscious mind. It has been widely suggested that from the moment of our birth everything that happens to us, every experience, everything we see, hear, touch, taste and smell, is recorded in our subconscious mind. Consciously, we have forgotten, but the subconscious mind does not forget. When, through the pendulum, we ask it for information, it can draw on this vast reservoir of knowledge in supplying an answer. Thus it can be argued that an answer supplied by the pendulum is likely to be more accurate than one consciously formulated. It is so because it is based on more information.

An interesting illustration lending some support to this concept was provided by a colleague of mine. At a party we were discussing the various ways in which the pendulum could be used. Belinda Hughes, my colleague, had previously mentioned a book which she had not read for years, but which was somewhere in her bookcase. This bookcase covered two walls of her lounge, reaching from wall to ceiling, and contained several thousand books. Apparently Belinda had no idea where the particular book was and, as our discussion was taking place in another room, she could not pick up any clues from her memory of what the book looked like. Through questioning with the pendulum Belinda decided it could be found in the west-wall bookcase, third shelf from the bottom, seventh book in from the left. She was nearly right. It was the fifth book from the left.

This is not an isolated example, and such occurrences are difficult to explain. Perhaps the theory that the pendulum is tapping a vast reservoir of subconscious knowledge may appeal to you. Perhaps not. However, you do not have to accept the theory in order to use the pendulum in helping you make decisions. See it simply as a very practical, quick means of banishing your indecision and relieving yourself of much needless worry.

USING THE PENDULUM

Faced with a decision to make, review the information you have and ask the pendulum what you should do. Let us imagine the weather is a little uncertain and you are wondering whether to wear light summer-weight clothes or warmer mid-weight garments. Look out of the window, listen to the weather report and pose your question: 'Is it advisable for me to wear summer-weight clothes today?' When you get an answer, you may care to check it by asking: 'Is it advisable for me to wear mid-weight clothes today?' Hopefully, your two answers should support each other, one 'yes' and one 'no'.

If you do not secure a clear answer, the reason usually lies in the way you have framed your question. It may not be sufficiently precise. Sometimes the pendulum will, in fact, tell you this by swinging diagonally, or by repeatedly indicating the 'I don't know' response. When this occurs, try reframing the question. As you become increasingly familiar with the pendulum and its movements, you will develop considerable confidence in its decision-making ability. Accordingly, when you fail to get the appropriate response, you will tend to look for some error in your own questioning rather than in the pendulum itself.

Sometimes the pendulum may seem to work better for you than it does on other occasions. Perhaps you might like to let it tell you when you are ready to make a decision by asking: 'Please indicate by a "yes" (or positive) reaction when I am ready to make my decision about which clothes I should wear today.' As mentioned above, maintain a detached attitude while you ask such questions. Once you get your positive reaction the way would seem clear for you to resolve your indecision. When you do so, put the decision into action and forget it. Do not waste time second-guessing, wondering what would have happened if the pendulum had made some other choice. The whole idea of using the pendulum is to turn off such useless agonizing, to spare you the worries of uncertainty which are probably far worse than the consequences of making the wrong decision.

You may find it interesting to experiment with your pendulum on the foods you eat. One method suggested by Hitching in *Pendulum: The PSI Connection*, is to hold the pendulum over the back of your free hand to get the reaction characteristic of you, and to then move your hand over the food. Any change in swing will indicate whether the food in question is harmful. In my own case I get a to-and-fro swing over my hand and if this 'yes' or positive movement continues when I have it over the food, I assume it is compatible with my system. If the swing changes to 'no' or negative, I assume the food is likely to be incompatible.

Alternatively, you might simply hold the pendulum over the food and pose the question: 'Is this food beneficial to me at this moment?' This is a useful method to use with food supplements such as vitamin tablets. The pendulum can tell you, first, whether you require the supplement at this time, and second, how many tablets to take.

If you are a gardener, you may follow a similar pattern. Hold the pendulum over a plant, note its movement, and then suspend it over the soil where you intend to place it. If the movement remains the same, you can be hopeful of good results. Should there be a change, a disharmony between plant and soil is likely. Adding fertilizer may correct this.

There are other possibilities, of course, for using the pendulum but I will not elaborate further. In the context of this chapter I will simply restate the key point. Indecision causes us to feel stressed, pressured, and makes our lives less pleasant than they would otherwise be. The pendulum provides a method of overcoming this problem. You may care to try it.

8. Building Positive Self-Concepts

Why do we behave the way we do? An answer to this question will help us understand ourselves more fully. Hopefully, if we are able to use this information we shall be better placed to assume more control of our own lives. The key word here is 'use'. Many psychiatrists are concerned with helping people achieve insight into their own behaviour, the assumption being that this will enable them to resolve their personal difficulties. The man who cannot express love is shown how his childhood environment suppressed his free expression of affection. With this understanding it is suggested to him that he is now able to overcome his early conditioning. As an adult he can cope with the situation because he thinks more maturely. Incidents seen as highly traumatic through the eyes of a child can be now viewed in a changed perspective, and once this is done, more appropriate behaviour follows. The man frees himself to express his love openly and fully. Sometimes it happens. Often it does not. The person involved learns to speak more intelligently about his problem, but his behaviour shows no change.

It is as I commented earlier (p. 6): possession of knowledge about ourselves is one thing; using it to improve our lives is something else again. We have this knowledge or, if we do not, we can acquire it from books such as this one. Once we have it, we must apply it. It is not enough to think: 'Yes, that's right. I do act like that. Now I understand why I did such a stupid thing. I must really do something about it', and leave it at that. You have to take action. No magician exists who can banish your problems with a wave of his magic wand. You have to help yourself. In the pages of this book are contained simple, straightforward ways of doing so. They work. Whether they help you or not depends on your willingness to use them.

A BASIC NEEDS EXPLANATION OF BEHAVIOUR

So back to an explanation of behaviour. We do things because they satisfy some basic need within us. The most obvious of such needs are physiological. We eat because we are hungry, we sleep because we are tired. The place in which we sleep and the particular food we eat are products of the culture in which we live. We learn certain ways of gratifying our needs, but the basic motivation is always the same. In fact, the most effective way of persuading someone to do something is to raise in him a need and then show him how, by following a certain course of action, he will be able to achieve its satisfaction.

As well as the physiological needs of hunger, thirst, sex and sleep, we desire safety. Normally we think of this in physical terms, of shelter and protection. Psychological safety can be very important too. Often we play safe in human relationships, never risking any deep involvement because there is always the chance we might be hurt. This is why self-disclosure is difficult. Our need for psychological safety may be so strong that it prevents us risking deep involvement with another human being. By so doing we miss the 'highs', the really ecstatic moments that for many people make life worth living. We do have this need for safety, it is just a matter of getting it in perspective. Surely we should behave in ways which protect ourselves physically and psychologically. Yet, taking the occasional risk does add spice and meaning to life.

The need to be loved and to belong also seems basic in human beings. I feel this is the most important element in a good marriage. To your marriage partner and children you are important. You have a place where you belong, where you are loved and cherished. Such a refuge seems very necessary in a world where we are so eminently replaceable. When recently I moved from one university to take up a position at another, I knew that the study which I left, my 'home' for the past six years, would soon have another name on the door. Another person would teach the courses I had taught and provide the 'ear' for student problems I had provided. Very soon it would be as if I had never existed in that particular place.

Closely associated with this need to be loved and to belong is that of esteem. It is important for each of us to feel we are of value. This is one of the great rewards of working in the helping professions. If someone comes to me, miserable and unhappy, and I am able to help him so he feels better in himself, I am enhanced. My self-esteem receives a tremendous boost. My existence has contributed to the happiness of another human being. I think that each of us needs to feel of value in some way and much of our behaviour can be explained as attempts to achieve this sense of personal worth. As Leo Rosten puts it: 'The purpose of life is to *matter*; to be productive, to be useful, to have it make some difference that you lived at all.'

Another need I would regard as basic is that of self-actualization. This term, coined by the American psychologist, Abraham Maslow, encompasses the need to develop all our potentialities as human beings so that we can become all that we are capable of becoming. Much of my own behaviour is readily explicable in terms of this need. Writing this book is an example. Naturally, I hope it is able to help many people. Yet, perhaps its greatest value is personal. It has helped me pull together so many ideas into a coherent framework. I have become more aware of the journey I have travelled towards self-actualization, and the avenues that are opening before me. I hope the ideas I have set down will help you in your own odyssey, for virtually everything I have written about has been discovered through my need to make the most of myself, to be everything I am capable of being.

A final need motivating much of our behaviour is that of knowing and understanding. It is the basis of our whole concept of education, with its emphasis upon intellectual skills. Much human behaviour can be explained in terms of this quest for knowledge. For many of you it is the reason for you reading this book. So the need to know takes its place with the physiological needs, the security, love and belonging needs, and the self-esteem and self-actualization needs, as a basic explanation of why we do the things we do. It is a relatively simple explanation. I see that as an advantage. Too often we lose ourselves in the complexities of explanations which defy our understanding. Do not be misled by the apparent simplicity, however. As you consider your own behaviour you will find countless examples supporting the appropriateness of this basic needs approach. In fact, I would simplify it further by suggesting that all human behaviour may be explained in terms of one fundamental need, that of maintaining the concept we have of ourselves.

SELF-CONCEPT AS AN EXPLANATION OF BEHAVIOUR

I, like so many people, am an admirer of Charles Schultz and his 'Peanuts' comic strip, believing he is a very perceptive practical psychologist. Charlie Brown, one of his greatest creations, is the epitome of a person possessing what I would describe as a negative self-concept. He is stupid. This is a fact he accepts. He is a loser who believes with complete certainty that everything he attempts will end in failure. I would suggest that if a person perceives himself negatively, this concept will determine his future behaviour. Conversely, if a person has a positive feeling about himself, he will expect to be successful in life. I believe that for the most part, we tend to get what we expect. Success breeds further success; failure breeds further failure.

I have used the term 'self-concept' several times already. It is a shorthand way of encompassing the sum total of an individual's view of himself. This includes all those aspects of the environment to which we refer when we say 'I' or 'me'. It is an abstraction, of course. We cannot hold our self-concept in our hands and say: 'Look, here it is.' It is simply a convenient way of speaking about something that would otherwise be very vague and difficult to understand.

Still, the way we see ourselves does have tremendous reality. For example all of these statements could be part of a person's self-concept: 'I am happy.' 'I am a loser.' 'I am beautiful.' 'I am bad.' 'I am a gossip.' 'I am lovable.' 'I am a slow learner.' 'I am neurotic.' You may notice that this list contains not only attributes but also values placed upon them. This is something we all do. Not only would you consider yourself as a mother or father, but also as good, bad or mediocre in this role. Clearly, in the self-concept of any one person, there will be much contradictory information. Still, an overall feeling about oneself is normally present. One thinks of oneself either in a predominantly positive way: 'I'm all right', or in a predominantly negative way: 'I'm really not worth much.'

There is a compelling sense of reality about the self-concept which is not limited only to aspects of yourself. It can extend to your tennis or football team. You can identify with it so strongly that its wins elate you and its losses depress you. Its successes are your successes and its failures are your failures.

Certainly this was true of Merle Holding, the wife of one of my tennis partners, Barry. She was a rabid football fan and the fortunes of her team affected not only herself, but Barry too. If her team lost, she was so miserable for the following week that she made Barry's life virtually unbearable. This showed up in his tennis. I used to dread playing with him after his wife's team lost, because he was terrible. His concentration was poor, he had a 'defeated' attitude, and physically he was sluggish and slow. But when Merle's team won she gave Barry such a great time that the difference in his play was incredible. He was a different person. This is not really an extreme example, and I expect many readers will find it familiar.

Self-concept, too, embraces the family unit as a whole. Families draw together under attack. If your daughter is critized, you react negatively because your self-concept embraces your family – it is part of you. An attack upon any family member is an attack upon you, a critical judgement passed on you. Thus the self-concept is far more than just physical characteristics, although the way we look is very influential in the opinion we hold of ourselves.

Obesity is one such characteristic. Fred Ingram, in his younger days, was an excellent athlete, fit and lean. At this time his self-concept was very positive. He thought well of himself as a person. As he grew older he exercised less and ate more. His consumption of alcohol rose considerably. The inevitable weight increase accompanied by a thickening waistline lead to changes in Fred's self-concept. He saw himself in a much less favourable light. Because of his obesity his speed of movement was reduced. He tired easily. Hot weather distressed him. Generally, he began thinking of himself as a has-been, old, over the hill, and he behaved accordingly. In his work as an insurance salesman, he lost his zest, his drive. Turning on the charm became too much of an effort. Life became rather a bore.

It is easy to see, in this case, the all-pervasive effect exerted by the concept Fred now held of himself. All aspects of his life were affected. Although he consulted me about his general loss of energy and his frequent feelings of depression, it seemed the way I could be of most help would be in encouraging him to lose weight. Using the method of mental imagery and suggestion outlined in chapter 4, Fred 'saw' himself the way he wanted to be, telling himself that this change would actually take place. By so doing he reduced his weight to the level he desired. As a result he regained his previous, positive self-concept and behaved in accordance with it. So never underestimate the importance of physical appearance.

Maxwell Maltz, in his best-selling *Psycho-cybernetics*, has confirmed this through his long experience as a plastic surgeon. He documents the amazing changes that took place in patients whose appearance was altered. Shy, retiring people became more outgoing and confident as a result of quite minor cosmetic surgery. Because they felt happier about their appearance they liked themselves more as people and began behaving in quite different ways. It is possible, then to change your self-concept, and by so doing change your behaviour. Yet this is not always as easy to accomplish as these examples would suggest.

Much psychological literature would suggest that our self-concept is firmly established during the first seven or eight years of life and that change after that time is usually quite minor. If this is true, that we achieve a stable self-concept so early in life, a tremendous responsibility is placed upon parents to influence this in a positive direction. Once established it provides a screen through which virtually all incoming information is filtered. That is, we tend to accept things which match up with our existing self-concept and either ignore or distort those which contradict it. This is why change is normally so difficult to achieve.

CONSTANCY OF THE SELF-CONCEPT

Because the self-concept provides a filter through which we view the world, it determines our behaviour by the way in which we strive to maintain inner consistency. Barbara Fullarton was leaving the suburb in which she had lived for the past six years and moving interstate. When several of her neighbours heard the news, in one way or another, they indicated how pleased they were about her departure. Barbara's self-concept was basically positive, she saw herself as a worth-while person. This incoming information contradicted this because here were people who did not value her. To maintain the consistency of her inner view of herself she regarded such comments as jokes, not meant to be taken seriously. In this way her self-concept could remain intact. Her interpretation may have been correct: her neighbours may have been joking. If they were not, she had distorted incoming information in such a way that no pressure existed for her to change the concept she held of herself.

The self-concept is very selective in its determination of how experiences are perceived. John Anderson is in Form 3 at his local secondary school. He regards himself as a failure. During a mathematics lesson, one of his teachers says to him: 'John, you worked that last problem really well.' To the teacher's surprise, John's response is quite hostile. The teacher is stunned. Why had John reacted like this? Seen from the child's viewpoint, his reaction makes sense. He is a failure, no good at school work, yet here is a person telling him he has done something well. John knows he cannot do things well. Obviously the teacher is trying to make fun of him. Aggressively he rejects the comment, and by so doing, protects himself against the necessity of modifying his self-concept to embrace the fact that he might be able to succeed with mathematics problems. Fortunately the teacher persisted in his positive remarks, gradually blunting John's hostility until the boy could accept the possibility that he might be capable of success. Such acceptance preceded a gradual improvement in his self-concept.

The self-concept we hold generates a set of expectancies. Sue is an adolescent, and due to the quick rate of growth which normally occurs at this time of life, she is rather clumsy. Her family frequently comment upon this clumsiness, sometimes in a joking way and other times with exasperation. Frequently she is ridiculed for her ineptness. As a result Sue expects to keep bumping into things because she accepts she is a clumsy person. Accordingly, when asked to help serve visitors during a family dinner party, she knows she is going to do something clumsy. She fulfils her own expectations by spilling soup over one of the guests.

HOW WE ACQUIRE OUR SELF-CONCEPTS

From the above example it becomes clear how we acquire a concept of ourselves. It is not something with which we are born. Rather, we learn it from other people who are important to us, such as parents, peers and teachers. We learn how other people react to us, whether we are liked or unliked, acceptable or unacceptable. Laura Huxley in *You Are Not The Target*, explains it this way: 'What brings about self-rejection? There are many causes; one of the most significant is that many people reject themselves for the illogical but emotionally compelling reason that they were once rejected by someone else.'

Early suggestion can fix a pattern in our minds, that we are 'this way' or 'that way'. This mental image becomes deeply embedded as part of our self-concept and our behaviour reflects it. The person who ruefully admits to being a hopelessly inept handyman, who cannot handle tools, is quite likely to have received such comments as: 'You'll break that. Watch what you're doing. Get away from those tools. Can't you do anything right? You don't know anything about tools and you'll never learn to use them properly.'

As we have seen in past chapters, the power of suggestion is enormous. This is particularly true for children who are in such a vulnerable position. The suggestions they are given by those upon whom they are dependent shape their lives. They provide the raw material from which the self-concept is constructed and, as we have seen, this in turn controls future behaviour.

It is not only a matter of what we are told about ourselves. How we are told is also very important. If someone who matters to you tells you he loves you, this is a highly positive experience as long as you feel it to be true. However, if a mother says to her child: 'Of course Mother loves you dear', but speaks through clenched teeth and a body taut with annoyance, the words are unlikely to carry much conviction. Psychologists claim that approximately 70 per cent of the meaning of any message is carried by non-verbal means such as facial expression and body language generally. When words and body do not match up, it is the latter which is believed. The old adage: 'Don't do as I do, do as I say' neatly makes the point. If we cannot embody our message in our own behaviour, we delude ourselves·if we really believe that what we say is going to carry any weight at all. Practise what you preach and there is a good chance that you will achieve the result you wish. If you are unwilling to do so, you will probably waste your time and that of the person at whom the message is directed.

CHANGING THE SELF-CONCEPT

If you desire to change your self-concept in a positive direction, there are a number of ways you can go about it. The way you think about yourself, your mental self-image, is a result of your past experiences of success and of failure. You cannot change this but you can change the meaning that you attach to these past experiences. Viewpoints can change. You do not have to continue looking at things the way you did when you were much younger.

One way of improving your self-concept is to re-interpret the past. Dwell on your successes and forget the failures. Relive the former through mental imagery, recapture the feelings you had then, and transfer these feelings to a situation in which you wish to succeed at the present time. This helps you develop a success mentality. If you find it difficult to forget the failures, do some image-changing during your relaxation periods. First, relive the experience as you remember it happening. Then, using your power of imagination, change it to conform to the way you would have liked it to be. Reinforce this with positive affirmations: 'I can be a success. I will be a success. I am a success.' This may prove difficult at first. In our society it is not considered appropriate to praise yourself. Though self-humiliation and admission of inadequacy is acceptable, it is somehow wrong to suggest that you have done something well. Resist this negative influence and try some self-congratulation. You will find it valuable.

The value of such statements, oft-repeated, is that you condition your subconscious mind to accept them as truth. Then they become true for you. It is just another example of the use of positive thinking. That is really what the self-concept is all about. If you are thinking positive thoughts, your concept of yourself will be success-oriented. If you tell yourself negative things, you ensure your self-concept will be failure-oriented. In *The Magic Of Thinking Big*, David Schwartz has said: 'You are what you think you are. Think more of yourself and there is more of you.' In one sentence he has given us the key to improving our self-concept.

Another approach to achieving this goal is through the modifying of your own behaviour. You establish a target behaviour. In the present case this is to increase the number of positive thoughts you have about yourself. Several steps are involved. The first of these is self-observation. For a period of one week you monitor your thought processes, recording the number of positive and negative thoughts you have about yourself. If the former predominate over the latter, your self-concept is already reasonably sound, and you may wish to go no further. If the reverse is the situation for you, move on to the next step.

This involves changing your external environment by:
1. *Altering the cues that precede your behaviour*. For instance, if you normally have many negative thoughts after being in contact with certain people, try to organize things so that you avoid them as much as possible. This may not be easy as the world seems to be full of people eager to tell us why the actions

we might want to take can lead only to dreadful consequences. You know how enthusiastic you can sometimes be, bounding out to tell someone about the fantastic thing you are going to do, only to be thoroughly deflated by all the objections raised. So, if you want to develop a more positive self-concept, avoid the 'nay-sayers'.

2. *Altering the immediate consequences of your behaviour.* This will involve getting the co-operation of your family and friends, so that every time you express a positive thought about yourself you are rewarded, perhaps by praise or attention. Such reinforcement should increase the behaviour you want, especially if no one listens to you when you speak negatively. This is, of course, a most effective way of modifying not only your own behaviour but also that of other people. When they do as you wish, reward them, make them feel good. When they behave in ways which are not what you want, ignore them.

Terry Damon quarrelled violently with his wife. Not that this was unusual. It happened rather frequently. After some time passed, Terry felt guilty about his behaviour, and felt he should do something to make amends. His wife, Judy, loved flowers, so he bought her some and presented them to her when he returned home after work. Judy was delighted. Yet, next day, they again argued. Perhaps the flowers were not such a great idea, thought Terry. Really, it was not the actual flowers but the timing of their presentation that was the problem. What Terry had done was reward Judy for the arguing behaviour. He had, in fact, strengthened the very thing he wanted to eliminate.

A preferable course of action would have been to ignore Judy while she was argumentative and aggressive, or at least not reward her, but to provide the flowers after they had experienced a good time together. Perhaps they had made love very satisfyingly, or had shared enjoyable conversation and a meal beautifully prepared by Judy. Rewarding someone for positive behaviour is likely to increase that behaviour, yet so often this is the activity we ignore. We do not let others know when we appreciate the good things they are doing for us. So reward this positive behaviour and watch it increase. You will reap tremendous benefits.

The third step in the procedure is to alter your internal environment. This you do by:

1. Altering preceding cues.

One way of doing this is to tuck a small piece of white card under the wristband of your watch. On every occasion you check the time you will see it, reminding you to think something positive about yourself.

2. Reinforcing yourself immediately.

Have a store of happy experiences from the past available for use, times when you felt really marvellous. Think about one of these as an immediate reward whenever you have a positive thought about yourself.

This particular approach might sound cumbersome, but it is quite easy to put into practice. Undertaken as a family exercise, it can be very effective in improving the quality of life in the home. I realize, though, my insistence on positive thinking is open to at least one serious objection.

Whenever I speak about ways of improving self-concept, someone in the audience will always bring up the dangers of encouraging people to become completely egotistical, so completely full of themselves they will be impossible to live with. It is a risk. Everything we do, I suppose, has its risks. In this case, it is one I am prepared to take for I feel, in our society, that most people are more inclined to put themselves down than to exalt themselves. 'I'm not much good' is a more common self-concept than 'I'm the greatest'. Even if the latter opinion was held by more people, I wonder how serious a problem it would be. Many of the great achievements of this world seem to have been the work of people with sublime confidence in their own ability.

Is it so wrong to like yourself? Is it so wrong to love yourself? Eric Fromm in *The Art Of Loving* obviously does not think so:

The idea expressed in the Biblical 'love thy neighbour as thyself' implies that respect for one's own integrity and uniqueness, love for and understanding of one's own self, cannot be separated from respect and love and understanding for another individual. The love for my own self is inseparably connected with love for any other being.

I agree with Fromm. Until you can learn to love yourself, you will find it difficult to love anyone else. Once you do come to terms with yourself, accepting your strengths and weaknesses as part of you, yet still loving yourself as a unique human being, you provide a model for others. You demonstrate in the way you live your life what others can become if they would but shake off the fetters of negative thinking and self-doubt. We learn, I believe, mainly by imitation, so the person with a positive self-concept can provide a valuable model for others. I can see great virtue in a self-confident expectation of success; I can see little in a self-doubting expectation of failure. As Alexander Dumas put it: A person who doubts himself is like a man who would enlist in the ranks of his enemies and bear arms against himself. He makes failure certain by himself being the first person to be convinced of it.

9. The Achievement of Happiness

DO YOU WANT TO CHANGE?

What is happiness? Different people would answer this question in different ways. There are no prescriptions for universal happiness, but some of the more effective paths are explored in this chapter. All are based on the belief that happiness comes from inside us. Usually we seek happiness in the wrong place. It is not something external, outside ourselves. It comes from within. All of us, I believe, have a great potential for happiness. In too many of us, this remains undeveloped because we do not realize its existence. We are, within rather broad limits, responsible for our own happiness. Accepting this viewpoint may not be easy. It means we must change ourselves if we are dissatisfied with our present state. No one else can do it for us. It is so much easier to blame our environment, other people, for our misery, than to blame ourselves and do something about it. In one of his many articles, Carl Rogers has pointed out that:

The dilemma of our unhappiness lies within us. Our irritability, our nagging, our whining, and all the other ways our negative emotions are channelled – all these prevent us from owning our emotions. The key to resolving the dilemma of emotions is simply to *own* them – that is, to own up to the fact that these emotions and behaviour are ours, that *we are creating them*, and that all the blaming in the world will help us not one iota. The only way to get over whining, nagging and jealousy is to own up to them and then decide to work on ourselves to change ourselves – not others. [Author's italics.]

Are you prepared to change? If so, some of the ideas that follow should help you develop increased happiness independently of your environment. Instead of letting outward

133

events, such as traffic jams, bad weather, and other people dictate your emotions, you will be able to develop an internal control. As has been pointed out repeatedly, circumstances alone do not make us happy or unhappy. It is the way we react to circumstances that determines our feelings. You can choose to do the things that make you feel good about yourself rather than the things that make you feel bad.

But will you do so, I wonder? As you read this chapter, you might think that it, along with earlier ideas, solves all your problems. You finish the book, perhaps try some of the ideas out for a day or two, lose the first flush of enthusiasm, forget your good intentions, and remain unchanged. I really hope this will not happen. Reading about achieving happiness, gaining knowledge that is new to you, is only the beginning. To change yourself you have to *do* something, to take action. Perhaps there are too many new ideas spread before you, and you ask yourself: 'Where will I start?' You may then look around for more information to help you decide, thus postponing action further. It does not really matter where you begin. Take a quick decision and get started.

This, incidentally, is pertinent to increased happiness. In any situation, make a decision quickly, then stop thinking about it. As has been pointed out above (p. 114), most decisions with which we are faced are either relatively unimportant, so that any of the actions we contemplate will be all right, or they are such that lengthy consideration is unlikely to improve upon them. So make a decision now and plunge into your self-improvement immediately. Remember that the longest journey begins with but a single step.

TAKE ACTION GRADUALLY

When you take action, after your firm decision, do not try to accomplish everything at once. If you decide you are going to improve your marriage relationship, do not decide you will be an absolute paragon of virtue, doing everything right, being unfailingly cheerful and helpful, giving your mate everything he or she needs for sublime contentment. Be more realistic.

Start by making small changes, setting up a series of short-term goals which you can achieve on a step-by-step basis. Some of these might involve reducing the amount of nagging you do, avoidance of critical comments, and playing down your attempts to change your partner. As well as making such reductions, try increasing your appreciative comments, being more courteous, and paying him or her the little attentions you know are enjoyed.

Perhaps you might use each of these as a sub-goal, deciding that, just for one day you will be very appreciative and non-critical. Then you might try it for two days out of each week and so on. Each time you achieve your sub-goal, or sub-sub-goal, you will feel a sense of satisfaction and the exciting anticipation of the next step. Always you will be moving towards your long-term goal of increased happiness through an improved marital relationship. If you take action in this way, you will feel much more content in yourself – for anticipation is usually more fun than the actual achievement. When you know you are making progress towards a goal you will feel a sense of elation. After you attain your end point, though pleased with what you have achieved, you soon take it for granted and it loses its zest. With the step-by-step approach, you will always be in a state of anticipation, every achievement being succeeded by thought of the next advance to be made. Happiness is not only a station you arrive at; it also lies in the way you travel.

AVOID SELF-BLAME

Do not blame yourself if you make mistakes and have relapses. This is to be expected. We cannot remake ourselves overnight. For every few forward steps we take, we may slip back a step or two. Overall, though, we gradually move on towards our goals. You will feel better taking action, doing something positive even if some things do not turn out the way you expect. You win some, you lose some, but as you keep trying the percentage of successes will increase. Do not let the disappointment affect you so you sink back into lethargy, unwilling to experiment.

Above all, do not *blame* yourself, for this is completely negative and unhelpful. Part of the oriental genius for contentment is the ability to accept failure without regret, regarding it placidly as part of life's eternal fabric. This seems a healthy approach for us all to take. You will not get the best out of life unless you take action on the knowledge you have. If this does not produce the result which you want, try again. None of us really fails — we just give up trying, and by so doing deprive ourselves of potential happiness.

Refusing to blame yourself for mistakes has other benefits too. You can give up the idea of being perfect, for if this is a goal you establish for yourself, you ensure your own unhappiness. Human beings are not perfect and cannot be so. If you insist you should be perfect, you continually blame yourself for not living up to your own unrealistic expectations. A complete no-win situation. You just punish yourself and that is no way to achieve increased happiness. Why judge yourself at all? Accept yourself as a human being, prone to error. Refuse to *rate* yourself as a person and do not interpret the judgements of other people as ratings either. Evaluate your performance, and encourage others to do likewise if you so desire, but whether you do something well or poorly is not a measure of your worth as a human being. You are valuable and worthwhile in yourself through the very fact of your existence. Do not permit a judgement of your performance to diminish this intrinsic value. It can be very damaging if you do, as Jan and Mike Hosking found out.

Jan's sexual relationship with Mike, her husband, had been steadily deteriorating over the past two years. During the previous five years of marriage they had both enjoyed each other physically, but now a sense of boredom had set in. Both Jan and Mike put sex well down their list of priorities and by so doing were losing the sense of closeness and intimacy they once shared. Jan would not go to bed at night until the house was spotless, the floors clean, the kitchen immaculate, the ironing completed. For his part, Mike gradually drifted into the habit of spending more and more time in his home workshop. He considered finishing a certain project more important than sitting talking with Jan, that is if he could get her to sit down for long enough.

A sexual relationship is more than intercourse. It involves touching affectionately, enjoying each other's company and sharing experiences. This takes time. Two people need to be with each other, unpressured by other 'duties', so that they can relate to each other. In bed together may be the best time for this, particularly when children make privacy difficult. With Jan and Mike other things took precedence and they were usually too tired to talk together when they finally went to bed. There was little time for talking and sex was a chore, often avoided with relief on both sides.

Realizing they were drifting apart, Jan and Mike decided to do something about it. They would restore their sexual relationship to its previous splendour. The way they set about this was rather unfortunate, seeing it as a matter of performance. Their goal was simultaneous orgasm. The one problem with this sort of approach is the tendency to focus on how well you are doing instead of on what you are doing. This usually leads to poor performance, whatever the task might be. Both Jan and Mike were overly concerned with the actions they should take to ensure that a simultaneous orgasm took place. They were also haunted by the thought of how awful it would be if they failed to achieve this.

Under these conditions they virtually ensured failure. They made love under conditions of high anxiety, a condition extremely disruptive to sexual performance. Their initial failure increased the anxiety and strain, making future success unlikely. Mike, in fact, had periods of impotence for the first time in his life and Jan was unable, on most occasions, to achieve an orgasm at all. Both partners experienced feelings of diminished self-worth. They judged themselves harshly, not confining their criticism to: 'I am a failure at achieving simultaneous orgasm with my partner during sexual intercourse', but generalizing to: 'I am a failure as a person because my performance is so bad.'

The point I wish to stress is that you must maintain your feelings of self-worth despite the fact that you may be doing some things badly. The measure of you as a person is not determined by how well or how badly you do something. Jan and Mike's initial problem of sexual boredom was aggravated by the way they went about solving it. They could not dissociate their own failure from their overall sense of personal worth. If they had been able to do so, they would have been more able to reject the one thing that had not worked and try a different approach. They had been operating under the assumption that couples have to work at making their sexual relationship a success. Masters and Johnson, in their research into human sexuality, have demonstrated very clearly that setting up sex as a task is the one thing you should not do.

Couples seeking greater sexual happiness need less, not more, deliberate direction in their efforts. An improved physical relationship will occur more readily within an overall context of increased trust, vulnerability and emotional openness. Feelings cannot be forced. They must unfold in their own way and in their own time. Communication between husband and wife is all important. By words, by touch, by eye contact, each must tell the other what he or she feels, needs, wants. This is a gradual process of unfolding, needing quiet time together, so a couple can share themselves, touching and talking. Sometimes words are unnecessary, closeness coming from lying side by side sharing a silence. From such sharing comes deep sexual intimacy, welling up naturally, effortlessly, in its own time.

ENJOY THE PRESENT MOMENT

Sharing in this way helps you to enjoy the present moment, a thing that many of us have forgotten or have never known how to do. Perhaps we have never learned to keep our thinking in the present to produce enjoyment.

Because it is possible to turn your thinking in any direction you wish, you can determine to keep your attitude and thinking calm and cheerful *right now,* at this very moment. Do this and your happiness will increase greatly. If, as suggested earlier (p. 66), it is the journey that is important rather than the destination, your concentration on the 'now' for its own sake will help you enjoy life more fully. Make the present moment a successful experience for it is the only time we have to be happy. Do not lose your opportunity to do so by always looking for something in the future, expecting that good things may be just around the corner. Make the good things happen now and the future will look after itself.

Our reluctance to live in the present moment is sometimes due to a suspicion that we are missing out on something. It is easy to feel that not only is life a party going on with other people somewhere else, but that we have not even been invited. At some time or another most of us have probably felt this way. There is some truth in it too. Our life experiences are only one sample of the range of possible experiences we might have. We cannot do everything so we are doing some things and not others. If we constantly dwell on all the wonderful things we may be missing out on, we make ourselves miserable for no gain and at considerable cost. It seems preferable to concentrate on what we *are* doing, and finding in it as much pleasure as possible, thus making ourselves much happier.

Also, of course, where opportunities to sample new things come, we try these as well. Concentration on enjoyment of the present moment will contribute to increased efficiency. We are unable to do everything but we are able to do some things, and it seems unproductive to let the things we cannot do interfere with those we can do. The wise man does not allow his enjoyment of the present moment to suffer because other people might be doing something else.

Look upon happiness as a thing called *now,* and you will find that you talk with a smile. Laughter will come readily as you live in the present, and this smooths your path. A day on which you have found no reason to laugh is a bleak day indeed, for a man without mirth is like a wagon without springs – he is jolted disagreeably by every pebble in the road. Such jolting does not make for happiness and laughter helps you cope with the minor irritations in life which, if you allow them, can be so annoying. It is so important to your general enjoyment of life to emancipate yourself from petty irritations. If you tear a button off your shirt while dressing hurriedly, it is not really of earth-shattering importance. If it makes you feel better, swear about it, then forget it. Do not carry it with you to spoil your day. Laugh at your foibles and they will never interfere with your happiness.

HAPPINESS AS PLEASANT THINKING

Attempting to define happiness in a way that is acceptable to everyone is probably an impossible task. It means something different to each of us. I see it as a state of mind in which most of our thinking is pleasant. When we let our minds drift back into the past, it is towards happy incidents. As we live in the 'now', we focus on the enjoyable elements in the present situation. When we contemplate the future it is with optimism and a confident expectancy that it will bring good things. This may not be your interpretation of happiness, but it is the one that has guided much of what I have written. Accordingly I have stressed the control you have to direct your thoughts into the channel you desire.

Personally, I find no joy in constantly thinking about my troubles unless there is some point in me doing so. If I can improve my situation, then there is gain in such thinking. But if I cannot, if my thoughts are just running around like squirrels in a cage, I prefer to think of more pleasant matters. I deliberately switch my thoughts to things which make me feel happier. It seems to me that the intelligent action to take is to be as happy as circumstances permit, and if you find it upsetting to contemplate the ills of the world, you have the freedom to think about something else instead.

Thus it is a good idea to turn your attention outward, away from yourself, when you find the present moment made miserable by the direction your thoughts are taking. By concentrating on some external object you distract yourself from your introspective self-punishment. This is why happiness may be promoted through the possession of a skill in which you can take pride, belief in a cause, absorption in a hobby, or friendly interest in other people. All these take you outside yourself. Through absorption in the external activity you can forget yourself.

THE IMPORTANCE OF WORK

Work is perhaps the most obvious of these external interests.

Yet, it is so easy to convince yourself that you do not like work. Often there is a good reason, for some jobs do entail a monotony and repetition that is difficult to combat. However, many people who change jobs with relative frequency still dislike work intensely, thus generating a continual flow of negative emotions which preclude happiness. Possibly this attitude is due to the Protestant ethic that differentiated work and play so sharply. Work was good for the soul, it was man's duty to labour, and it kept him out of trouble. Having time for play was dangerous, nothing constructive was being done, so it was condemned as the work of the devil. The concepts of work and enjoyment never came together, which is unfortunate, for it is possible to combine the two. Some people live for their work. This is hard on their families, but their job does provide such a tremendous source of enjoyment that time devoted to it is pleasure. We do not have to go to such extremes, but it is certainly worth the effort to treat it as a friend rather than as an enemy.

When you can take pride in work well done you have uncovered another source of happiness. Persistence in the anti-work attitude can make life a misery, for most of us have to spend so many hours a day earning a living. By co-operating with the inevitable, the fact that you do have to spend these hours in some form of work, it is then possible to focus on ways of making your labours more enjoyable. Happiness often lies not in doing what you like, but in liking what you do. The ability to maintain a daily interest in your work, to have a great enthusiasm, to regard each day as important, all these contribute to successful living. I would emphasise *daily* here. Again, it is taking one day at a time and concentrating on the present moment within each day that is important to your emotional well-being. Do not think of doing the same job, day in day out, for the next twenty, thirty, forty or fifty years. Such a vista would probably depress us all, but anyone can do and enjoy his work for this one day. That is all that matters – this day which is yours to enjoy if you choose to do so.

Ian Galloway, when he rises each morning, thinks of the day stretching before him, considering the circumstances of this time period as his environment. The attitude he takes is that, through the use of his mind, he has to fashion out of this particular environmental material a happy, cheerful day. He sees the day as full of materials for him to use, to create positive feelings, to achieve positive goals. Unlike many others, he does not see it as comprising a series of problems, obstacles, and anxiety-producing situations. Ian did not always think this way. It took a heart attack and a bout of depression before he came to this personally revitalizing concept of how to regard his working day. Hopefully, those of you who are reading this book will be able to adopt a positive outlook without the necessity of enduring either a heart attack or a depressive episode.

Look on the ways work is desirable. It can, as mentioned previously, redirect your thoughts away from personal trouble. Normally it can prevent boredom, if you allow yourself to become absorbed in what you are doing. If you wish, you can see it as a way of making holidays more enjoyable, on the theory that unless there were clouds we would not enjoy the sun. A negative view, perhaps, but not so if it helps you more easily find enjoyment in your work. It provides the opportunity for success and accomplishment, be it ever so minor. After all, much of our happiness in life comes from a series of small triumphs rather than one or two thunderous successes. The sense of satisfaction derived from exercising your skill can cause a warm glow, likely to endure for long periods of time. Man's essential needs can, in fact, probably be reduced to three key essentials: something to do, something to look forward to, and someone to love. Work provides one means of satisfying at least the first two of these if your attitude towards it is a positive one.

Perhaps, despite all this, you still see work as boring. Yet, Fritz Perls, the founder of gestalt therapy, said that: 'Boredom involves a deliberate act of paying attention to something that is uninteresting and resolute withholding of attention from something else that would involve excitement.'

An academic colleague of mine, Frank Trinder, has certainly taken Perls' message to heart. He loathed meetings, seeing them as a cumbersome, time-consuming way of coming to trivial decisions. Boredom settled heavily upon him as he sat through the endless long-winded verbal barrages. Occasionally he said something himself. Frank's problem was that he took the biblical injunction: 'He who hath knowledge spareth his words' to heart, so his points were made briefly. Obviously, then, he spent a lot of time being rather inactive. That is, until he transferred his attention to the interactions between the other participants in the meeting. He became interested in the patterns. When Dr A. spoke, Professor B. usually responded critically. Why? When Mr C. advanced a proposal, Dr D. and Professor E. invariably supported him. Frank started to anticipate who would speak next, and whether their statements would be positive or negative. He started analysing the reasons participants advanced for their viewpoints. Very quickly he became aware that these academically respectable arguments often concealed personal animosities and emotionally based prejudices. To Frank, the previously boring meetings became quite interesting, and he did learn a great deal about human nature.

There is an important general point illustrated by Frank's behaviour. When we are doing something which is affecting us negatively, the sensible thing is to stop, and do something else instead. This may be impossible. Frank had to attend the meetings. So, if we cannot change what we are doing, the next best thing is to change our attitude to what we are doing. That is what Frank did. His environment had not changed, only his attitude to the environment.

BROADEN YOUR RANGE OF INTERESTS

You can achieve such satisfaction in other ways, too, primarily by having a wide range of interests. Once work for the day has been completed, it is normally wise to forget it, transferring your attention to other activities using quite different mental and physical faculties. This is Bennett's idea of a 'day within a day' which was described in chapter 6 on using time efficiently. In this way you maintain a freshness of outlook.

You may wish to deliberately plan for such diversity, resolving to start something new each week, such as reading an unfamiliar book, planting a garden bed, buying clothes, visiting an unfamiliar beauty spot, or embarking on a different hobby. For many people, this is a most effective antidote to psychosomatic illness. Without a hobby, our leisure time can hang heavy on our hands, so that our minds are more and more apt to dwell on our troubles.

A wide range of interests, be they hobbies, sports or anything else, is also a wonderful way of easing a person from employment into retirement. This can reduce the accompanying trauma that can make this time of life so difficult.

Jack Salisbury had worked ever since he left school at fourteen. Now, at sixty-five, he looked forward to days of lazing around, doing nothing. No pressures, no demands, just pleasing himself. It was a pleasant thought, far more appealing as an idea than it turned out to be in reality. To a man whose waking hours had once been filled with work-oriented activities, time hung heavy. Now, he drifted, unable to think of things to do to help the hours pass. Jack was bored. At sixty-seven he was dead. Perhaps there was no connection, but the frequency with which this pattern occurs suggests that unless you prepare for retirement well before the actual date upon which you finish work you are unlikely to enjoy longevity. The secret seems to lie in the development of a wide range of interests in your fifties, if you have not already done so by this time. Then, when one interest, work, drops out, you have much to take its place.

In *The Art of Selfishness,* David Seabury has suggested that you combine past, present and future orientations to make your later years fulfilling. Use retrospection, looking back into the past to identify those things you have enjoyed doing. Perhaps you can do them again. Or those things you would have liked to do, but never seemed to have time for. Maybe some of them can be done now in the absence of time pressure. Use introspection, too, to analyse the present. Each day eliminate one or two things that cause you discontent, and find two or three things which give you satisfaction. Even prospection can be of value, looking forward into the future, thinking of the enjoyable things you can do in your old age once the pressures are off, once the 'shoulds' and 'musts' lose their strength.

The points made above apply equally strongly for a woman once her family has grown up and left home. If she has made care of family her lifetime's work, developing little interest in other activities, she is likely to feel that her useful life is over. Once we feel this way, that we no longer have a purpose in life, our health tends to deteriorate. It would seem that having something to do is the most effective way of enjoying long life. You need to feel there is some point in your existence.

DEVELOPING A PURPOSE IN LIFE

An entire system of therapy – logotherapy – has been constructed on this single premise. Victor Frankl, its founder, explains, in *Man's Search For Meaning,* how he came to a realization that the pursuit of meaning is central to man's life. Imprisoned in one of Hitler's concentration camps during the Second World War, Frankl, a psychiatrist, studied his fellow-inmates. This, he explains, was to prevent him dwelling on his own misfortune. He was intrigued with the question of survival. Why did some prisoners, healthy, strong and fit, succumb very quickly to the hardships of concentration camp life while others, frail and ill, lived on year after year?

Having a reason to live was the answer, according to Frankl. Those who bemoaned their fate, continually asking: 'Why was I victimized? Why me? Why should I suffer?' tended to die quickly. They saw no point in their suffering. The survivors saw some meaning in their ordeal. They were undergoing purification so they would be better prepared for future great deeds, they were extirpating the guilt of past evil, they were absolving their loved ones from shame. It did not seem to matter how fanciful the reasons were to an outsider, it was the prisoner's own belief that was important. If he could convince himself there was some meaning to his suffering, his chances of survival were high.

After his release, Frankl developed logotherapy as a cohesive system around the basic tenet that people can gain relief from despair through having a task to fulfil. This is because despair is suffering behind which the sufferer sees no meaning. But meaning may be found in more varied forms than the sufferer realizes and this is the therapist's task. He has to broaden the patient's horizons, exposing him to the full range of meaning possibilities. Above all, meaning can be found in accepting the unavoidable and turning it into a challenge, creating something good out of something bad. Turning defeat into victory makes life particularly meaningful. Demonsthenes, the Greek orator, for example, stuttered badly as a youth. Determined to overcome this impediment he spent hours walking along the shore, his mouth full of small stones while he spoke aloud. This single-minded practice produced a beautifully modulated speaking voice, the envy of his contemporaries.

Consider a more common illustration, that of the elderly man, who, filled with grief over the death of his loved wife, feels that his existence is finished. Unless he finds a new meaning in life, it is likely that he will follow his wife very quickly. This may be what he prefers, but life goes on for most of us. Picking up the pieces, we can find new interests, a new purpose in our existence. When man functions as a goal-striver he tends to be happy most of the time.

Yet, we must take life one step at a time, not looking for the grandiose plan but for the challenges of the moment. If we are unable to find such challenges, we need to create them for ourselves or else we wither and die. We must set up tasks to accomplish so we can feel the thrill of achievement. Once we do this we become purposeful and goal-oriented, active and vital. Conversely, if we think life is purposeless, meaningless, that a human being is nothing more than an insignificant speck of dust lost in the immense universe, we drift into boredom, lethargy and inactivity.

You can choose your attitude. You can set up the daily tasks and challenges that will make your life meaningful. Do this and you will also gain in self-knowledge. 'How can we learn to know ourselves?' wrote the German philosopher, Goethe. 'Never by reflection, but by action. Try to do your duty and